# A CRITIQUE OF PURE TOLERANCE

ROBERT PAUL WOLFF

BARRINGTON MOORE, JR.

HERBERT MARCUSE

BEACON PRESS    BOSTON

"Beyond Tolerance" copyright © 1965
    by Robert Paul Wolff
"Tolerance and the Scientific Outlook"
    copyright © 1965
    by Barrington Moore, Jr.
"Repressive Tolerance" copyright © 1965
    by Herbert Marcuse
"Postscript 1968" copyright © 1969
    by Herbert Marcuse
Library of Congress catalogue card number 65-20788
*All rights reserved*
Beacon Press books are published under the auspices
    of the Unitarian Universalist Association
Printed in the United States of America
First published by Beacon Press in 1965
First published as a Beacon Paperback in 1969
Robert Paul Wolff gratefully acknowledges permission
to reprint a passage from *The Loyal and the Disloyal* by
Morton Grodzins, copyright © 1956 by the University
of Chicago.

*International Standard Book Number:* 0–8070–1559–8

*9 8 7 6*

# CONTENTS

# FOREWORD

THE authors apologize for the title which they have lightly yet respectfully plagiarized. Their small book may contain some ideas that are not alien to Kant. More than modesty makes us refer to a footnote in the *Critique of Pure Reason:* "the 'I think' expresses the act of determining my existence." We like to apply this sentence not as Kant did here to the transcendental subject only, but also to the empirical one.

The first essay is by a philosopher steeped in the analytical tradition, an authority on Kant, and, if interested in social theory and history, allergic to any emanations from the spirit of Hegel. The last essay is also by a philosopher, an authority on Hegel, who considers the contemporary analytical tradition dangerous, where it is not nonsense. The author of the middle essay is a sociologist trained in a tradition that regarded all philosophy as absurd and dangerous. That we have managed to produce a book together is in itself some small tribute to the spirit of toleration.

Inhabitants of the larger Cambridge academic community, we often met and as friends passionately argued some of the issues discussed in the following pages. Some time ago we agreed to set down our thoughts about tolerance and its place

in the prevailing political climate. Though we
have read and pondered one another's writings,
and modified our own views according to our
respective degrees of stubbornness, we have not
sought in any way to merge them. The reader
will have no difficulty in finding where we dis-
agree.

On the other hand, from very different starting points and by very different routes, we ar-
rived at just about the same destination. For each
of us the prevailing theory and practice of tolerance turned out on examination to be in varying
degrees hypocritical masks to cover appalling
political realities. The tone of indignation rises
sharply from essay to essay. Perhaps vainly, we
hope that readers will follow the steps in the
reasoning that produced this result. There is,
after all, a sense of outrage that arises in the head
as well as the heart.

R. P. W.
B. M.
H. M.

# BEYOND TOLERANCE

BY ROBERT PAUL WOLFF

THE virtue of a thing, Plato tells us in the *Republic*, is that state or condition which enables it to perform its proper function well. The virtue of a knife is its sharpness, the virtue of a racehorse its fleetness of foot. So too the cardinal virtues of wisdom, courage, temperance, and justice are excellences of the soul which enable a man to do well what he is meant to do, viz., to live.

As each artifact or living creature has its characteristic virtue, so too we may say that each form of political society has an ideal condition, in which its guiding principle is fully realized. For Plato, the good society is an aristocracy of merit in which the wise and good rule those who are inferior in talents and accomplishment. The proper distribution of functions and authority is called by Plato "justice," and so the virtue of the Platonic utopia is justice.

Extending this notion, we might say, for example, that the virtue of a monarchy is loyalty, for the state is gathered into the person of the king, and the society is bound together by each subject's personal duty to him. The virtue of a

military dictatorship is honor; that of a bureaucratic dictatorship is efficiency. The virtue of
traditional liberal democracy is equality, while
the virtue of a socialist democracy is fraternity.
The ideal nationalist democracy exhibits the virtue of patriotism, which is distinguished from
loyalty by having the state itself as its object
rather than the king.

Finally, the virtue of the modern pluralist
democracy which has emerged in contemporary
America is TOLERANCE. Political tolerance is that
state of mind and condition of society which enables a pluralist democracy to function well and
to realize the ideal of pluralism. For that reason,
if we wish to understand tolerance *as a political
virtue*, we must study it not through a psychological or moral investigation of prejudice, but by
means of an analysis of the theory and practice of
democratic pluralism.

My purpose in this essay is to understand the
philosophy of tolerance as well as to subject it
to criticism. I have therefore devoted the first
section entirely to an exposition of the concept
as it is related to the theory of pluralism. In the
second section, I explore several possible arguments for tolerance, and try to exhibit the theory
of democratic pluralism as the product of a union
of opposed conceptions of society and human
nature. Only in the final section is the theory subjected to the criticisms which, in my opinion,
make it ultimately indefensible in the contemporary age. This may at first seem a needlessly
roundabout way of proceeding. I have adopted
it because I see pluralism not as a thoroughly

mistaken theory, but rather as a theory which played a valuable role during one stage in America's development and which has now lost its value either as description or prescription. In that sense, the present essay urges that we transcend tolerance, and as Hegel reminds us, the process of transcendence is as much an incorporation as it is a rejection.

I

Like most political theories, democratic pluralism has both descriptive and prescriptive variants. As a description, it purports to tell how modern industrial democracy—and particularly American democracy—really works. As a prescription, it sketches an ideal picture of industrial democracy as it could and should be. Both forms of the theory grew out of nineteenth century attacks on the methodological individualism of the classical liberal tradition.

According to that tradition, political society is (or ought to be—liberalism is similarly ambiguous) an association of self-determining individuals who concert their wills and collect their power in the state for mutually self-interested ends. The state is the locus of supreme power and authority in the community. Its commands are legitimated by a democratic process of decision and control, which ensures—when it functions properly—that the subject has a hand in making the laws to which he submits. The theory focuses exclusively on the relationship between the individual citizen and the sovereign state. Associations other than the state are viewed as secondary in importance and dependent for their existence on the pleasure of the state. Some liberal philosophers counsel a minimum of state interference with private associations; others argue for active state intervention. In either case, non-governmental bodies are relegated to a subsidiary place in the theory of the state. The line of dependence is traced from the people, taken as an aggregate of unaffiliated individuals, to the state, conceived as the embodiment and representative of their collective will, to the private associations, composed of smaller groupings of those same individuals but authorized by the will of the state.

Whatever the virtues of classical liberalism as a theory of the ideal political community, it was very quickly recognized to be inadequate as a portrait of the industrial democracy which emerged in the nineteenth century. The progressively greater divergence of fact from theory could be traced to two features of the new order. The first was the effective political enfranchisement of the entire adult populations of the great nation-states; the second was the growth of an elaborate industrial system in the private sphere of society, which gave rise to a new "pluralistic" structure within the political framework of representative government.

Traditional democratic theory presupposed an immediate and evident relation between the individual citizen and the government. Whether in the form of "direct democracy," as Rousseau desired, or by means of the representative mechanism described by Locke, the state was to confront the citizen directly as both servant and master. The issues debated in the legislature would be comprehensible to every educated subject, and their relevance to his interests easily understood. With the emergence of mass politics, however, all hope of this immediacy and comprehensibility was irrevocably lost. The ideal of a small, self-governing, autonomous political society retained its appeal, finding expression in the utopian communities which sprang up in Europe and America throughout the nineteenth century. As a standard by which to judge the great industrial democracies of the new era, however, it suffered from the greatest possible failing—irrelevance. Permanent, complex institutional arrangements became necessary in order to transmit the "will of the people" to the elected governors.

At the same time, great industrial corporations appeared in the economic world and began to take the place of the old family firms. As labor unions and trade associations were organized, the classical picture of a market economy composed of many small, independent firms and a large, atomized labor supply, became less and less useful as a guide to economic reality. Individuals entered the marketplace and came in contact with one another through their associations in groups of some sort. The state in its turn brought its authority to bear on the individual only indirectly, through the medium of laws governing the behavior of those groups. It became necessary to recognize that, both politically and economically, the individual's relation to the state

was mediated by a system of "middle-size" institutional associations.

The size and industrial organization alone of
the modern state destroy any possibility of classical liberal democracy, for the intermediating
bureaucratic organizations are necessary whether
the economy is private and capitalist or public
and socialist in structure. In addition, however,
three factors historically more specific to the
American experience have combined to produce
the characteristic form which we call pluralism.

The first factor, in importance as well as in
time, is the federal structure of the American system. From the birth of the nation, a hierarchy of
local governments, formerly sovereign and autonomous, interposed itself between the individual and the supreme power of the state. The
United States, as its name implied, was an association of political communities rather than of
individuals. The natural ties of tradition and
emotion binding each citizen to his native colony
were reinforced by a division of powers which
left many of the functions of sovereign authority
to the several states. Hence the relation of the
individual to the federal government was from
the beginning, and even in theory, indirect and
mediated by intervening bodies. Furthermore, as
the eighteenth century debates over unification
reveal, the constitution took form as a series of
compromises among competing interests—large
states versus small, agriculture versus commerce,
slave-holding versus free labor. The structure of
the union was designed to balance these interests,
giving each a voice but none command. The

conception of politics as a conflict of more or less permanent groups was thus introduced into the foundation of our government. By implication, an individual entered the political arena principally as a member of one of those groups, rather than as an isolated agent. Conversely, the government made demands upon the individual and responded to his needs, through the intercession of local authorities. As the volume of government activity grew throughout the nineteenth and twentieth centuries, this federal structure embedded itself in countless judicial and executive bodies. In America today, it is impossible to understand the organization of education, the regulation of commerce, or the precise allocation of responsibility for law enforcement without acknowledging the historically special relationship of the states to the federal government.

A second factor which has shaped the character of American democracy is our oft-chronicled penchant for dealing with social problems by means of voluntary associations. This phenomenon was made much of by Tocqueville and has since been portrayed by students of American politics as our peculiar contribution to the repertory of democratic techniques. It seems that whereas some peoples turn to God when a problem looms on the social horizon, and others turn to the state, Americans instinctively form a committee, elect a president and secretary-treasurer, and set about finding a solution on their own. The picture is idealized and more than a trifle self-congratulatory; it evokes images of the prairie or a New England town meeting, rather than a dirty industrial slum. Nevertheless, it is a fact that a remarkable variety of social needs are met in America by private and voluntary institutions, needs which in other countries would be attended to by the state. Religion, for example, is entirely a non-governmental matter because of the prohibition of an established church. The burdens of primary and secondary education are borne jointly by local governments and private institutions; higher education is dominated by the great private universities and colleges with state institutions of any sort only recently playing a significant role. The subsidy and encouragement of the arts and letters has been managed by the great charitable foundations, and until the advent of military research and development, the natural sciences found their home solely in the laboratories of universities and private industry. In addition to industry, agriculture, religion, education, art, and science, countless other dimensions of social activity have been organized on the basis of voluntary, non-governmental associations.

In order to clarify the relationship between the government and this network of private associations, we must first observe that while some groups perform their function and achieve their goal directly, others are organized as pressure groups to influence the national (or local) government and thus achieve their end indirectly. Needless to say, most associations of the first sort engage in political lobbying as well. Nevertheless, the distinction is useful, for it enables us to identify the two principal "pluralist" theories of the relationship between group and government. The first, or "referee" theory, asserts that the role of the central government is to lay down ground rules for conflict and competition among private associations and to employ its power to make sure that no major interest in the nation abuses its influence or gains an unchecked mastery over some sector of social life. The most obvious instance is in the economic sphere, where firms compete for markets and labor competes with capital. But according to the theory a similar competition takes place among the various religions, between private and public forms of education, among different geographic regions, and even among the arts, sports, and the entertainment world for the attention and interest of the people.

The second theory might be called the "vector-sum" or "give-and-take" theory of government. Congress is seen as the focal point for the pressures which are exerted by interest groups throughout the nation, either by way of the two great parties or directly through lobbies. The laws issuing from the government are shaped by the manifold forces brought to bear upon the legislators. Ideally, congress merely reflects these forces, combining them—or "resolving" them, as the physicists say—into a single social decision. As the strength and direction of private interests alters, there is a corresponding alteration in the composition and activity of the great interest groups—labor, big business, agriculture. Slowly, the great weathervane of government swings about to meet the shifting winds of opinion.

More important than federalism or interest-group politics in fostering the ideology of pluralism has been the impact on the American consciousness of religious, ethnic, and racial heterogeneity. Many of the original colonies were religiously orthodox communities, deliberately created in order to achieve an internal purity which was unattainable in the hostile political climate of England. The Reformation split Europe first into two, then into many, warring camps, and it was quite natural to view the nation as an association of religious communities rather than of individuals. Where some compromise could be achieved among the several sects, as eventually occurred in England, political society became in a sense a community of communities. In the United States, the deliberate prohibition of an established church made it necessary to acknowledge a diversity of religious communities within the nation. Eventually, this acceptance of heterogeneity was extended to the Roman Catholic community, and then even to the Jews.

The ethnic diversity brought about by the great immigrations of the nineteenth century produced a comparable effect in American life. The big cities especially came to be seen as agglomerations of national enclaves. Little Italies, Chinatowns, Polish ghettos, German communities, grew and flourished. America became a nation of minorities, until even the descendants of the original settlers acquired an identifying acronym, WASP.

The ethnic and religious communities in American society encountered one another through the pluralistic mechanisms of politics and private associations which already existed. The typical "hyphenated" community (Italian-American, Polish-American, etc.) had its own churches, in which the religious practices of the old country—special saints, holy days, rituals—were kept up. There were newspapers in the mother tongue, men's clubs, folk societies, businessmen's associations, trade union branches, all based on the ethnic or religious unity of the local community.

The religious and ethnic groups entered the political system at the precinct, city, or county level, using the unified mass of their voting populations as a weight to be thrown on the political scales. The decentralized, hierarchical federal structure of American government was perfectly suited to ethnic politics. The first matters of social importance which impinged on the consciousness of the group were, typically, of a sort that could be decided at the level of city government, where only a rudimentary organization and political knowledge was necessary. As Italian, Irish, Polish, or Jewish politicians ascended the ladder of elective office, they encountered the larger, multi-ethnic and multi-religious community. There they acted first as spokesmen for their own kind, and later as statesmen capable of acknowledging the greater public good.

If we draw together all these descriptive fragments, we have a portrait of pluralist democracy. America, according to this account, is a complex interlocking of ethnic, religious, racial, regional, and economic groups, whose members pursue their diverse interests through the medium of private associations, which in turn are coordinated, regulated, contained, encouraged, and guided by a federal system of representative democracy. Individual citizens confront the central government and one another as well through the intermediation of the voluntary and involuntary groups to which they belong. In this way, pluralist democracy stands in contrast to classical democracy of the liberal model; indeed, it is curiously like feudal society, in which the individual played a political role solely as a member of a guild, incorporated town, church, or estate rather than as a subject *simpliciter*. As in medieval political society, so in pluralist democracy, the guiding principle is not "one man—one vote" but rather, "every legitimate group its share." In modern America, it is taken for granted that a rough equality should be maintained between labor and business or among Catholics, Protestants, and Jews. The fact that "labor" constitutes the overwhelming majority of the population or that there are ten times as many Catholics as Jews is rarely seen as a reason for allotting influence in those proportions.

Pluralism is a theory of the way modern industrial democracies work, with particular applicability to the United States; it is also an ideal model of the way political society ought to be organized, whether in fact it is or not. As a descriptive theory, pluralism requires empirical verification, of the sort which hosts of political scientists have sought to provide in recent decades. As a normative theory, however, pluralism must be defended by appeal to some principle of virtue or ideal of the good society. In the history of the discussion of pluralism three distinct sorts of justification have been offered.

The earliest argument, dating from the pre-industrial period of religious conflict between Catholics and Protestants, Nonconformists and Anglicans, asserts that the toleration of divergent religious practices is a necessary evil, forced upon a society which either cannot suppress dissidence or else finds the social cost of suppression too high. Orthodoxy on this view is the ideal condition, intolerance of heresy even a duty in principle. It is now an historical commonplace that the great Anglo-American tradition of religious liberty can be traced to just such a grudging acceptance of *de facto* heterodoxy and not to early Protestant devotion to the freedom of individual conscience.

The second argument for pluralism presents it as a morally neutral means for pursuing political ends which cannot be achieved through traditional representative democracy. In this view, the ideal of democracy is a citizen-state, in which each man both makes the laws and submits to them. The political order is just and the people are free to the extent that each individual plays a significant and not simply symbolic role in the political process of decision. But for all the rea-

sons catalogued above, genuine self-government
is impossible in a large industrial society organized along classic democratic lines. The gulf is
so broad between the rulers and the ruled that
active citizen participation in the affairs of government evaporates. Even the periodic election
becomes a ritual in which voters select a president whom they have not nominated to decide
issues which have not even been discussed on
the basis of facts which cannot be published.
The result is a politics of style, of image, of faith,
which is repugnant to free men and incompatible
with the ideal of democracy.

But decisions will be taken, whether by democratic means or not, and so some other way
than elections must be found to submit the rulers
to the will of the ruled. Pluralism is offered as
the answer. Within the interest groups which
make up the social order, something approxi-
mating democracy takes place. These groups, in
turn, through pressure upon the elected representatives, can make felt the will of their members and work out the compromises with opposed interests which would have been accomplished by debate and deliberation in a classical
democracy. The government confronts not a
mass of indistinguishable and ineffectual private
citizens, but an articulated system of organized
groups. Immediacy, effectiveness, involvement,
and thus democratic participation are assured to
the individual in his economic, religious or ethnic
associations—in the union local, the church, the
chapter of the American Legion. Control over
legislation and national policy is in turn assured

to the associations through their ability to deliver votes to the legislator in an election. The politician, according to this defense of pluralism, is a middleman in the power transactions of the society. He absorbs the pressures brought to bear upon him by his organized constituents, strikes a balance among them on the basis of their relative voting strength, and then goes onto the floor of the Congress to work out legislative compromises with his colleagues, who have suffered different compositions of pressures and hence are seeking different adjustments of the competing social interests. If all goes well, every significant interest abroad in the nation will find expression, and to each will go a measure of satisfaction roughly proportional to its size and intensity. The democratic ideal of citizen-politics is preserved, for each interested party can know that through participation in voluntary, private associations, he has made his wishes felt to some small degree in the decisions of his government. To paraphrase Rousseau, the citizen is a free man since he is at least partially the author of the laws to which he submits.

The first defense of pluralism views it as a distasteful but unavoidable evil; the second portrays it as a useful means for preserving some measure of democracy under the unpromising conditions of mass industrial society. The last defense goes far beyond these in its enthusiasm for pluralism; it holds that a pluralistic society is natural and good and an end to be sought in itself.

The argument begins from an insight into the

relationship between personality and society.
Put simply, the idea is that the human personality, in its development, structure, and continued functioning is dependent upon the social
group of which it is a significant member. The
influence of society upon the individual is primarily positive, formative, supportive—indeed,
indispensably so. The child who grows to man-
hood outside a social group becomes an animal,
without language, knowledge, the capacity to
reason, or even the ability to love and hate as
other men do. As the infant is reared, he inter-
nalizes the behavior patterns and evaluative attitudes of that immediate circle of adults whom
the sociologists call his primary group. A boy
becomes a man by imitating the men around him,
and in so doing he irrevocably shapes himself
in their image. The way he speaks and carries his
body, how he responds to pain or pleasure, the
pattern of his behavior toward women, old men,
children, the internal psychic economy of his
hopes and fears and deepest desires, all are primarily imitative in origin. Throughout life, the
individual seeks approval from his "significant
others," willing to submit even to death rather
than violate the mores he has learned. The standards and judgment of his society echo within
him as guilt or shame.

Those philosophers are therefore deeply mistaken who suppose that the social inheritance
is a burden to be cast off, a spell from which we
must be awakened. Without that inheritance, the
individual is exactly nothing—he has no organized core of personality into which his culture

has not penetrated. The most thorough radical is the merest reflection of the society against which he rebels. So we are all naturally, irremediably, beneficially, bound up with the social groups in which we locate ourselves and live out our lives.

Since man is by nature an animal that lives in a group, it is folly to set before ourselves as a political ideal a state whose members owe their sole allegiance to the state. A fusion of group loyalty with political obligation is possible only when the primary group is identical with the total society—in short, only in a utopian community like New Lanark or an Israeli kibbutz. In a large society, loyalty to the state must be built upon loyalty to a multiplicity of intrasocial groups in which men can find the face-to-face contacts which sustain their personalities and reinforce their value-attitudes.

Morton Grodzins summarizes this theory of "multiple loyalties" in his book, *The Loyal and the Disloyal:*

> The non-national groups, large and small, play a crucial, independent role in the transference of allegiance to the nation. For one thing, they are the means through which citizens are brought to participate in civic affairs and national ceremony. . . . In theory, at least, the chain is an endless one. For if the dictates of government are enforced by the sanctions of the smaller groups, the smaller groups in turn establish the governmental policies they enforce. This is one hallmark of democracy: populations effectuating the policies they determine. Where population groups believe—

or understand—this dual role, their patriotic performance is all the stronger. . . . Individuals, in short, act for the nation in response to the smaller groups with which they identify themselves. The larger group, the nation, need only establish the goal. The citizen may or may not participate in this goal definition, may or may not agree with it. Except in rare cases, he will nevertheless supply the force through which its achievement is attempted. His loyalty to smaller groups insures his doing it. They perforce must support its causes, especially when, as during war, the very existence of the nation is at stake. So it is that mothers tearfully send their unwilling sons to war. So it is that loyalties to smaller groups supply the guts of national endeavor, even when that endeavor has no meaning to the individual concerned.                                    (pp. 65-67)

To each defense of pluralism, there corresponds a defense of tolerance. In the would-be orthodox society, tolerance of diversity is a necessary evil, urged by the voices of reason against the passion of intolerant faith. So the *politiques* of France avoided a mortal civil war by the Edict of Nantes; so too modern Russia countenances Titoism in eastern European territories which it can no longer completely control. Such tolerance is not a virtue—a strength of the body politic—but a desperate remedy for a sickness which threatens to be fatal.

To the champion of pluralism as an instrument of democracy, tolerance is the live-and-let-live moderation of the marketplace. Economic competition is a form of human struggle (medieval warfare was another) in which each combatant simultaneously acknowledges the legitimacy of his opponent's demands and yet gives no quarter in the battle. A tension exists between implacable opposition on the one hand and mutual acceptance on the other. If either is lost, the relationship degenerates into cooperation in one case, into unconditional warfare in the other. The capacity to accept competing claims as legitimate is the necessary pre-condition of compromise. Insofar as I view my opponents as morally wrong, compromise becomes appeasement; if my own claims are unjust, I can press them only out of unwarranted self-interest. Tolerance in a society of competing interest groups is precisely the ungrudging acknowledgment of the right of opposed interests to exist and be pursued. This economic conception of tolerance goes quite naturally with the view of human action as motivated by interests rather than principles or norms. It is much easier to accept a compromise between competing interests—particularly when they are expressible in terms of a numerical scale like money—than between opposed principles which purport to be objectively valid. The genius of American politics is its ability to treat even matters of principle as though they were conflicts of interest. (It has been remarked that the genius of French politics is its ability to treat even conflicts of interest as matters of principle.)

Tolerance plays an even more important role in the third defense of pluralism, the one based upon a group theory of society and personality.

In a large society, a multiplicity of groups is
essential to the healthy development of the individual, but there is a danger in the emotional
commitment which one must make to his primary group. In the jargon of the sociologists,
out-group hostility is the natural accompaniment
of in-group loyalty. The more warmly a man
says "we," the more coldly will he say "they."
Out of the individual strength which each draws
from his group will come the social weakness
of parochial hatred, which is to say, intolerance.

One solution to the problem of intolerance,
of course, is to loosen the ties which bind the
individual to his ethnic, religious, or economic
groups. We are all brothers under the skin, is the
message of the humanist; which means the ways
in which we are alike matter more than the ways
in which we are unlike. But the danger of dis-
solving parochial loyalties is that without them
man cannot live. If the personality needs the re-
inforcement of immediate response, the face-to-
face confirmation of expectations and values, in
order to be strong, and if—as this theory claims—
no man can truly take a whole nation as his primary group, then it is disastrous to weaken the
primary ties even in the name of brotherhood.
To do so is to court the evils of "mass man," the
unaffiliated, faceless member of the lonely
crowd.

The alternative to the indiscriminate levelling
of differences in a universal brotherhood is tolerance, a willing acceptance, indeed encouragement, of primary group diversity. If men can be
brought to believe that it is positively good for

society to contain many faiths, many races, many styles of living, then the healthy consequences of pluralism can be preserved without the sickness of prejudice and civil strife. To draw once again on Plato's way of talking, pluralism is the condition which a modern industrial democracy must possess to function at all; but tolerance is the state of mind which enables it to perform its function well. Hence, on the group theory of society, tolerance is truly the virtue of a pluralist democracy.

## II

Thus far, I have simply been expounding the concept of tolerance, exhibiting its place in the theory of democratic pluralism. As we have seen, there are two distinct theories of pluralism, the first emerging from traditional liberal democratic theory and the second from a social-psychological analysis of the group basis of personality and culture. With each is associated a different notion of tolerance. In the first instance, tolerance is equated with the acceptance of individual idiosyncrasy and interpersonal conflict; in the second instance, tolerance is interpreted as the celebration of primary group diversity. I want now to raise the more difficult question, whether pluralism and tolerance in any of their forms are defensible ideals of democratic society and not simply useful analytical models for describing contemporary America.

The first, or instrumental, theory of pluralism is dependent for its justification on the earlier liberal philosophy from which it derives. If we wish to evaluate its fundamental principles, therefore, and not simply its effectiveness as a means for realizing them, we must go back to the doctrine of individualism and liberty, as expressed for example by John Stuart Mill, and consider whether it can be defended as an ideal of political society. In his famous and influential essay *On Liberty*, Mill defends the sanctity of the individual against what he sees as the unjustified interferences of society and the state. Mill portrays the individual Englishman in much the way that the tradition of English law portrays his home—as a sanctuary within which he may think as he wishes and act as he chooses, so long as his thoughts and actions do not invade the sanctuaries of his fellow citizens. In a classic statement of the liberal conception of the individual, Mill undertakes to distinguish between the private and public realms of action. He writes:

> There is a sphere of action in which society, as distinguished from the individual, has, if any, only an indirect interest: comprehending all that portion of a person's life and conduct which affects only himself or, if it also affects others, only with their free, voluntary, and undeceived consent and participation. . . . This, then, is the appropriate region of human liberty. It comprises, first, the inward domain of consciousness, demanding liberty of conscience in the most comprehensive sense, liberty of thought and feeling, absolute freedom of opinion and sentiment on all subjects, practical or speculative, scientific, moral, or theological. . . . Secondly, the principle requires

liberty of taste and pursuits, of framing the plan of our life to suit our own character, of doing as we like, subject to such consequences as may follow, without impediment from our fellow creatures, so long as what we do does not harm them, even though they should think our conduct foolish, perverse, or wrong. Thirdly, from this liberty of each individual follows the liberty, within the same limits, of combination among individuals; freedom to unite for any purpose not involving harm to others: the persons combining being supposed to be of full age and not forced or deceived.

Mill goes on to argue that even in the sphere of public-regarding actions, which fall outside this privileged inner sanctuary, society has a right to interfere with the individual only for the purpose of advancing the welfare of the society as a whole. That is to say, within the private sector, society has no right at all of interference; within the public sector, it still has only the *possibility* of such a right, conditional upon the existence of a utilitarian justification. For Mill and the classical libertarian philosophy, then, tolerance is the readiness to respect the inviolability of the private sphere of the individual's existence. A man may choose to wear strange clothes, grow a beard (or shave one off, if others wear them), practice unfamiliar religions, deviate from the sexual norms of his community, or in any other way reject the tastes and habits of society. The liberal philosophy demands that society refrain from interfering with his practices, either by legal or by informal social sanctions. What thus begins as a grudging acceptance of idiosyncrasy may hopefully flourish as the encouragement of individuality and the positive enjoyment of diversity.

In his public or other-regarding actions, the individual is of course held accountable by Mill, but it does not follow that he must completely bury his personal interests in the interest of society. Quite to the contrary, society itself, as the intersection of the public spheres of all the individuals who make it up, is a marketplace or battleground in which each individual pursues his private goals to the greatest extent compatible with the analogous pursuits by others. The only difference is that whereas in the private sector, society has no right at all to interfere with the individual's pursuit, because his actions have no influence upon the lives of others, in the common public sphere society imposes a rule of equity upon its members. Insofar as the mechanism of the marketplace functions efficiently, it will automatically achieve the mutual restrictions and limitations which justice and liberty require. Where the market fails, or in the case of non-economic matters, the state will step in and legislate the necessary regulation.

If we try to imagine a society in which the ideal of liberal tolerance is achieved in practice, what springs to mind is a large, cosmopolitan, industrial city, such as London or New York or Paris. The size, functional differentiation, speed of movement, fragmentation of social groupings, and density of population all cooperate to create a congenial setting for an attitude of easy

tolerance toward diversity of beliefs and practices. It is a commonplace that in the anonymity
of the big city one can more easily assemble the
precise combination of tastes, habits, and beliefs
which satisfy one's personal desires and then
find a circle of friends with whom to share them.
In the small town or suburb it is impossible to
escape from the sort of social interference in
private affairs which Mill condemned. But mere
size is not sufficient; the true liberation of the
individual requires that the city be diverse as
well. So the philosophy of tolerance, as expound-
ed by liberalism, leads naturally to an active encouragement of cultural, religious, social, and
political variety in an urban setting.

Like all political philosophies, the liberal theory of the state bases itself upon a conception
of human nature. In its most primitive form—
and it is thus that a philosophy often reveals itself best—liberalism views man as a rationally
calculating maximizer of pleasure and minimizer
of pain. The term "good," says Bentham, means
"pleasant," and the term "bad" means "painful."
In all our actions, we seek the first and avoid the
second. Rationality thus reduces to a calculating
prudence; its highest point is reached when we
deliberately shun the present pleasure for fear
of the future pain. It is of course a commonplace
that this bookkeeping attitude toward sensation
is the direct reflection of the bourgeois mer-
chant's attitude toward profit and loss. Equally
important, however, is the implication of the theory for the relations between one man and another. If the simple psychological egoism of lib-

eral theory is correct, then each individual must
view others as mere instruments in the pursuit
of his private ends. As I formulate my desires
and weigh the most prudent means for satisfy-
ing them, I discover that the actions of other
persons, bent upon similar lonely quests, may
affect the outcome of my enterprise. In some
cases, they threaten me; in others, the possibility
exists of a mutually beneficial cooperation. I ad-
just my plans accordingly, perhaps even enter-
ing into quite intricate and enduring alliances
with other individuals. But always I seek my own
pleasure (or happiness—the shift from one to the
other is not of very great significance in liberal
theory, although Mill makes much of it). For
me, other persons are obstacles to be overcome
or resources to be exploited—always means, that
is to say, and never ends in themselves. To speak
fancifully, it is as though society were an enclosed space in which float a number of spheri-
cal balloons filled with an expanding gas. Each
balloon increases in size until its surface meets
the surface of the other balloons; then it stops
growing and adjusts to its surroundings. Justice
in such a society could only mean the protection
of each balloon's interior (Mill's private sphere)
and the equal apportionment of space to all.
What took place within an individual would be
no business of the others.

In the more sophisticated versions of liberal
philosophy, the crude picture of man as a pleasure maximizer is softened somewhat. Mill recognizes that men may pursue higher ends than
pleasure, at least as that feeling or sensation is

usually understood, and he even recognizes the possibility of altruistic or other-regarding feelings of sympathy and compassion. Nevertheless, society continues to be viewed as a system of independent centers of consciousness, each pursuing its own gratification and confronting the others as beings standing-over-against the self, which is to say, as *objects*. The condition of the individual in such a state of affairs is what a different tradition of social philosophy would call "alienation."

Dialectically opposed to the liberal philosophy and speaking for the values of an earlier, pre-industrial, age is the conservative philosophy of community. The involvement of each with all, which to Mill was a threat and an imposition, is to such critics of liberalism as Burke or Durkheim a strength and an opportunity. It is indeed the greatest virtue of society, which supports and enfolds the individual in a warm, affective community stretching backwards and forwards in time and bearing within itself the accumulated wisdom and values of generations of human experience.

The fundamental insight of the conservative philosophy is that man is by nature a social being. This is not simply to say that he is gregarious, that he enjoys the company of his fellows, although that is true of man, as it is also of monkeys and otters. Rather, man is social in the sense that his essence, his true being, lies in his involvement in a human community. Aristotle, in the opening pages of the *Politics*, says that man is by nature a being intended to live in a political community. Those men who, by choice, live outside such a community are, he says, either lower or higher than other men—that is, either animals or angels. Now man is like the animals in respect of his bodily desires, and he is like the angels in respect of his reason. In a sense, therefore, liberalism has made the mistake of supposing that man is no more than a combination of the bestial and the angelic, the passionate and the rational. From such an assumption it follows naturally that man, like both beasts and angels, is essentially a lonely creature.

But, Aristotle tells us, man has a mode of existence peculiar to his species, based on the specifically human faculty for communication. That mode of existence is society, which is a human community bound together by rational discourse and shared values. Prudence and passion combine to make a rational pleasure calculator, but they do not make a man.

The conservative figure whose work contrasts most sharply with Mill's is the French sociologist Emile Durkheim. In a seminal study of social integration entitled *Suicide*, Durkheim undertook to expose the foundations of the individual's involvement with his society by examining the conditions under which that involvement broke down in the most dramatic way. Durkheim discovered that proneness to suicide was associated, in contemporary western society, with one of two sorts of conditions, both of which are parts of what Mill calls "liberty." The loosening of the constraints of traditional and group values creates in some individuals a condition of lawlessness, an absence of limits on desire and ambition. Since there is no intrinsic limit to the quantity of satisfaction which the self can seek, it finds itself drawn into an endless and frustrating pursuit of pleasure. The infinitude of the objective universe is unconstrained for the individual within social or subjective limits, and the self is simply dissipated in the vacuum which it strives to fill. When this lack of internal limitation saps the strength and organization of the personality beyond bearable limits, suicide is liable to result; Durkheim labels this form of suicide "anomic" in order to indicate the lawlessness which causes it.

Freedom from the constraint of traditional and social values brings with it a loss of limits and the abyss of anomie, according to Durkheim. (Note that the term "anomie," as originally defined by Durkheim, does *not* mean loneliness, loss of a sense of identity, or anonymity in a mass. It means quite precisely a-nomie, or lack of law.) Freedom from the constricting bonds of an intimate social involvement brings with it a second form of psychic derangement, called by Durkheim "egoism," which also leads in extreme cases to suicide. Durkheim sees the human condition as inherently tragic. The individual is launched upon an infinite expanse, condemned to seek a security which must always pass away in death and to project meaning into a valueless void. The only hope is for men to huddle together and collectively create the warm world of meaning and coherence which impersonal nature cannot offer. Each of us sees himself reflected in the other selves of his society, and together we manage to forget for a time the reality beyond the walls. Erik Erikson captures this sense of the besieged community in his discussion of the Russian character, in *Childhood and Society*. Erikson is portraying the traditional Russian peasant community as it appears in the opening scenes of a moving picture of Maxim Gorky's youth. Erikson writes:

> At the beginning there is the Russian trinity: empty plains, Volga, balalaika. The vast horizons of central Russia reveal their vast emptinesses; and immediately balalaika tunes rise to compassionate crescendos, as if they were saying, "You are not alone, we are all here." Somewhere along the Volga broad river boats deliver bundled-up people into isolated villages and crowded towns.
>
> The vastness of the land and the refuge of the small, gay community thus are the initial theme. One is reminded of the fact that 'mir', the word for village, also means world, and of the saying, "Even death is good if you are in the mir." A thousand years ago the Vikings called the Russians 'the people of the stockades' because they had found them huddling together in their compact towns, thus surviving winters, beasts, and invaders—and enjoying themselves in their own rough ways.
> (p. 318)

Durkheim marshalls statistics to show that where the intensity of the collective life of a community diminishes—as their "freedom," in Mill's sense, increases, therefore—the rate of suicide rises. Thus Protestant communities exhibit

higher rates than Catholic communities, which
in turn surpass the inward-turning Jewish communities. So too, education is "positively" corre-
lated with suicide, for although knowledge in
itself is not harmful to the human personality,
the independence of group norms and isolation
which higher education carries with it quite defi-
nitely is inimical. One might almost see in the
varying suicide rates a warning which society
issues to those of its number who foolishly ven-
ture through the walls of the town into the lim-
itless and lonely wastes beyond.

It seems, if Durkheim is correct, that the very
liberty and individuality which Mill celebrates
are deadly threats to the integrity and health of
the personality. So far from being superfluous
constraints which thwart the free development
of the self, social norms protect us from the dangers of anomie; and that invasive intimacy of
each with each which Mill felt as suffocating is
actually our principal protection against the
soul-destroying evil of isolation.

Needless to say, the dark vision of Durkheim
was not shared by all of the conservative critics
of liberal society, though more often than not
the inexorable advance of industrialism provoked
in them an extreme pessimism. In those who
wrote early in the century or even at the close
of the eighteenth century, there still lived a hope
that the traditional society of the preceding age
could be preserved. So we find Burke singing the
praises of the continuing community of values
and institutions which was England and damn-
ing the French revolution as an anarchic and

destructive deviation which could hopefully be corrected. Whether the critics of liberalism saw its advance as inevitable or as reversible, the more perceptive among them recognized in its espousal of tolerance the principal threat to the traditional society of shared values and communal integration. The very essence of social constraint is that one feels it as objective, external, unavoidable, and hence genuinely a limit beyond which one's desires may not extend. As soon as one enunciates the doctrine of the liberty of the internal life, those constraints become no more than suggestions—or, when backed by force, threats. But the individual is not capable of the self-regulation which Mill's doctrine of liberty presupposes. He is like a little child who ventures forth bravely to explore the playground but looks back every few moments to reassure himself that his mother is still there. So, we might say, evoking the images of traditional society, the adult ventures forth to explore life, secure in the knowledge that mother church and a paternal monarch will guide and support him. The recurrent use of familial metaphors in the description of social institutions expresses the dependent relationship which all men bear to their human community. Mill assures us in a number of passages that his principles of individual liberty are not meant to apply to children, who of course are not yet ready to assume the burden of freedom. What he fails to grasp, his conservative opponents seem to be telling us, is that men are the children of their societies throughout their lives. Absolute tolerance therefore has the same disastrous effects on the adult personality as extreme permissiveness on the growing child. In that sense, "progressive" theories of child-rearing are the true reflections of the liberal philosophy.

In the conflict between liberalism and conservatism, neither side can claim a monopoly of valid arguments or legitimate insights. The liberal apologists are surely correct in seeing traditional constraints as fetters which prevent the full development of human potentialities and tie men to unjust patterns of domination. What is more, the liberals at least are prepared to accept the burden of lost innocence which men bear in the modern age. To embrace traditions after their authority has been undermined is to retreat into an antiquarian refuge. It is absurd to decide on rational grounds that one will accept non-rational authority. There can be no turning back from the "liberation" of modern society, whatever one thinks of its desirability.

At the same time, the liberal assurance that the burdens of freedom can easily be borne is contradicted by the facts of contemporary life, as the conservative sociologists so clearly perceived. The elimination of superstition, on which the eighteenth-century *philosophes* counted so heavily and the liberation from social constraints for which Mill had such hopes are at best ambiguous accomplishments. The problem which forces itself upon the unillusioned supporter of liberal principles is to formulate a social philosophy which achieves some consistency between the ideals of justice and individual freedom on the one hand and the facts of the social origin and nature of personality on the other. Durkheim himself rejected any easy nostalgia for the communal glories of a past age. After demonstrating the correlation between education and suicide, he warned:

> Far from knowledge being the source of the evil, it is its remedy, the only remedy we have. Once established beliefs have been carried away by the current of affairs, they cannot be artificially reestablished; only reflection can guide us in life, after this. Once the social instinct is blunted, intelligence is the only guide left us and we have to reconstruct a conscience by its means. Dangerous as is the undertaking there can be no hesitation, for we have no choice. Let those who view anxiously and sadly the ruins of ancient beliefs, who feel all the difficulties of these critical times, not ascribe to science an evil it has not caused but rather which it tries to cure! . . . The authority of vanished traditions will never be restored by silencing it; we shall only be more powerless to replace them. . . . If minds cannot be made to lose the desire for freedom by artificially enslaving them, neither can they recover their equilibrium by mere freedom. They must use this freedom fittingly.                (p. 169)

Democratic pluralism, as it developed in the context of American life and politics during the late nineteenth and early twentieth century, purports to achieve just the required union of "liberal" principles and "conservative" sociology. As we saw in the first part of this essay, pluralism espouses a tolerance and non-interference in the private sphere which is precisely analogous to the classical liberal doctrine; however, the units of society between which tolerance and mutual acceptance are to be exercised are not isolated individuals but human groups, specifically religious, ethnic, and racial groups. All the arguments which Mill advanced in defense of the individual's right to differ from the surrounding society are taken over in pluralistic democracy as arguments for the right of a social group to differ from other social groups. At the same time, it is assumed that the individual will belong to some group or other—which is to say, that he will identify with and internalize the values of an existing infra-national community. We thus can see the implicit rationale for what is otherwise a most peculiar characteristic of pluralistic democracy, namely the combination of tolerance for the most diverse social groups and extreme intolerance for the idiosyncratic individual. One might expect, for example, that a society which urges its citizens to "attend the church or synagogue of your choice" would be undismayed by an individual who chose to attend no religious service at all. Similarly, it would seem natural—at least on traditional principles of individual liberty—to extend to the bearded and be-sandaled "beat" the same generous tolerance which Americans are accustomed to grant to the Amish, or orthodox Jews, or any other groups whose dress and manner deviates from the norm. Instead, we find a strange mixture of the greatest tolerance for what we might call established groups and an equally great intolerance for the deviant individual. The justi-

fication for this attitude, which would be
straightforwardly contradictory on traditional
liberal grounds, is the doctrine of pluralistic democracy. If it is good for each individual to con-
form to some social group and good as well that
a diversity of social groups be welcomed in the
community at large, then one can consistently
urge group tolerance and individual intolerance.

On this analysis, the "conservative liberalism"
of contemporary American politics is more than
merely a ritual preference for the middle of any
road. It is a coherent social philosophy which
combines the ideals of classical liberalism with
the psychological and political realities of modern pluralistic society. In America, this hybrid
doctrine serves a number of social purposes simultaneously, as I tried to indicate in my pre-
liminary discussion of the origins of pluralism.
It eases the conflicts among antagonistic groups
of immigrants, achieves a working harmony
among the several great religions, diminishes
the intensity of regional oppositions, and inte-
grates the whole into the hierarchical federal political structure inherited from the founding fa-
thers, while at the same time encouraging and
preserving the psychologically desirable forces
of social integration which traditional liberalism
tended to weaken.

### III

Democratic pluralism and its attendant principle of tolerance are considerably more defensible than either of the traditions out of which

they grow; nevertheless, they are open to a number of serious criticisms which are, in my opinion, ultimately fatal to pluralism as a defensible ideal of social policy. The weaknesses of pluralism lie not so much in its theoretical formulation as in the covert ideological consequences of its application to the reality of contemporary America. The sense of "ideological" which I intend is that adopted by Karl Mannheim in his classic study *Ideology and Utopia*, Mannheim defines ideology as follows:

> The concept 'ideology' reflects the one discovery which emerged from political conflict, namely, that ruling groups can in their thinking become so intensively interest-bound to a situation that they are simply no longer able to see certain facts which would undermine their sense of domination. There is implicit in the word "ideology" the insight that in certain situations the collective unconscious of certain groups obscures the real condition of society both to itself and to others and thereby stabilizes it.                                   (p. 40)

Ideology is thus systematically self-serving thought, in two senses. First, and most simply, it is the refusal to recognize unpleasant facts which might require a less flattering evaluation of a policy or institution or which might undermine one's claim to a right of domination. For example, slave-owners in the ante-bellum South refused to acknowledge that the slaves themselves were unhappy. The implication was that if they were, then slavery would be harder to justify. Secondly, ideological thinking is a denial

of unsettling or revolutionary factors in society
on the principle of the self-confirming prophecy
that the more stable everyone believes the situation to be, the more stable it actually becomes.

One might think that whatever faults the theory of pluralism possessed, at least it would be
free of the dangers of ideological distortion.
Does it not accord a legitimate place to all groups
in society? How then can it be used to justify
or preserve the dominance of one group over
another? In fact, I shall try to show that the
application of pluralist theory to American society involves ideological distortion in at least
three different ways. The first stems from the
"vector-sum" or "balance-of-power" interpretation of pluralism; the second arises from the
application of the "referee" version of the theory; and the third is inherent in the abstract theory itself.

According to the vector-sum theory of pluralism, the major groups in society compete
through the electoral process for control over
the actions of the government. Politicians are
forced to accommodate themselves to a number
of opposed interests and in so doing achieve a
rough distributive justice. What are the major
groups which, according to pluralism, comprise
American society today? First, there are the hereditary groups which are summarized by that
catch-phrase of tolerance, "without regard to
race, creed, color, or national origin." In addition there are the major economic interest
groups among which—so the theory goes, a
healthy balance is maintained: labor, business,

agriculture, and—a residual category, this—the consumer. Finally, there are a number of voluntary associations whose size, permanence, and influence entitle them to a place in any group-analysis of America, groups such as the veterans' organizations and the American Medical Association.

At one time, this may have been an accurate account of American society. But once constructed, the picture becomes frozen, and when changes take place in the patterns of social or economic grouping, they tend not to be acknowledged because they deviate from that picture. So the application of the theory of pluralism always favors the groups in existence against those in process of formation. For example, at any given time the major religious, racial, and ethnic groups are viewed as permanent and exhaustive categories into which every American can conveniently be pigeonholed. Individuals who fall outside any major social group—the non-religious, say—are treated as exceptions and relegated in practice to a second-class status. Thus agnostic conscientious objectors are required to serve in the armed forces, while those who claim even the most bizarre religious basis for their refusal are treated with ritual tolerance and excused by the courts. Similarly, orphanages in America are so completely dominated by the three major faiths that a non-religious or religiously-mixed couple simply cannot adopt a child in many states. The net effect is to preserve the official three-great-religions image of American society long after it has ceased to correspond to social reality and to discourage individuals from officially breaking their religious ties. A revealing example of the mechanism of tolerance is the ubiquitous joke about "the priest, the minister, and the rabbi." A world of insight into the psychology of tolerance can be had simply from observing the mixture of emotions with which an audience greets such a joke, as told by George Jessel or some other apostle of "interfaith understanding." One senses embarrassment, nervousness, and finally an explosion of self-congratulatory laughter as though everyone were relieved at a difficult moment got through without incident. The gentle ribbing nicely distributed in the story among the three men of the cloth gives each member of the audience a chance to express his hostility safely and acceptably, and in the end to reaffirm the principle of tolerance by joining in the applause. Only a bigot, one feels, could refuse to crack a smile!

Rather more serious in its conservative falsifying of social reality is the established image of the major economic groups of American society. The emergence of a rough parity between big industry and organized labor has been paralleled by the rise of a philosophy of moderation and cooperation between them, based on mutual understanding and respect, which is precisely similar to the achievement of interfaith and ethnic tolerance. What has been overlooked or suppressed is the fact that there are tens of millions of Americans—businessmen and workers alike—whose interests are completely ignored by this genial give-and-take. Non-unionized workers

are worse off after each price-wage increase, as
are the thousands of small businessmen who cannot survive in the competition against great na-
tionwide firms. The theory of pluralism does not
espouse the interests of the unionized against
the non-unionized, or of large against small business; but by presenting a picture of the American economy in which those disadvantaged ele-
ments do not appear, it tends to perpetuate the
inequality by ignoring rather than justifying it.

The case here is the same as with much ideological thinking. Once pluralists acknowledge
the existence of groups whose interests are not
weighed in the labor-business balance, then their
own theory requires them to call for an alteration of the system. If migrant workers, or white-
collar workers, or small businessmen are genuine *groups*, then they have a legitimate place in
the system of group-adjustments. Thus, pluralism is not explicitly a philosophy of privilege or
injustice—it is a philosophy of equality and justice whose *concrete application* supports inequality by ignoring the existence of certain
legitimate social groups.

This ideological function of pluralism helps
to explain one of the peculiarities of American
politics. There is a very sharp distinction in the
public domain between legitimate interests and
those which are absolutely beyond the pale. If
a group or interest is within the framework of
acceptability, then it can be sure of winning
some measure of what it seeks, for the process
of national politics is distributive and compro-
mising. On the other hand, if an interest falls

*outside* the circle of the acceptable, it receives
no attention whatsoever and its proponents are
treated as crackpots, extremists, or foreign
agents. With bewildering speed, an interest can
move from "outside" to "inside" and its partisans, who have been scorned by the solid and
established in the community, become presiden-
tial advisers and newspaper columnists.

A vivid example from recent political history
is the sudden legitimation of the problem of
poverty in America. In the post-war years, tens
of millions of poor Americans were left behind
by the sustained growth of the economy. The
facts were known and discussed for years by
fringe critics whose attempts to call attention to
these forgotten Americans were greeted with
either silence or contempt. Suddenly, poverty
was "discovered" by Presidents Kennedy and
Johnson, and articles were published in *Look*
and *Time* which a year earlier would have been
more at home in the radical journals which in-
habit political limbo in America. A social group
whose very existence had long been denied was
now the object of a national crusade.

A similar elevation from obscurity to relative
prominence was experienced by the peace movement, a "group" of a rather different nature.
For years, the partisans of disarmament labored
to gain a hearing for their view that nuclear war
could not be a reasonable instrument of national
policy. Sober politicians and serious columnists
treated such ideas as the naive fantasies of bearded peaceniks, communist sympathizers, and well-
meaning but hopelessly muddled clerics. Then

suddenly the Soviet Union achieved the nuclear parity which had been long forecast, the prospect of which had convinced disarmers of the insanity of nuclear war. Sober reevaluations appeared in the columns of Walter Lippmann, and some even found their way into the speeches of President Kennedy—what had been unthinkable, absurd, naive, dangerous, even subversive, six months before, was now plausible, sound, thoughtful, and—within another six months— official American policy.

The explanation for these rapid shifts in the political winds lies, I suggest, in the logic of pluralism. According to pluralist theory, every genuine social group has a right to a voice in the making of policy and a share in the benefits. Any policy urged by a group in the system must be given respectful attention, no matter how bizarre. By the same token, a policy or principle which lacks legitimate representation has no place in the society, no matter how reasonable or right it may be. Consequently, the line between acceptable and unacceptable alternatives is very sharp, so that the territory of American politics is like a plateau with steep cliffs on all sides rather than like a pyramid. On the plateau are all the interest groups which are recognized as legitimate; in the deep valley all around lie the outsiders, the fringe groups which are scorned as "extremist." The most important battle waged by any group in American politics is the struggle to climb onto the plateau. Once there, it can count on some measure of what it seeks. No group ever gets all of what it wants, and no *legitimate* group is completely frustrated in its efforts.

Thus, the "vector-sum" version of pluralist theory functions ideologically by tending to deny new groups or interests access to the political plateau. It does this by ignoring their existence in practice, not by denying their claim in theory. The result is that pluralism has a braking effect on social change; it slows down transformation in the system of group adjustments but does not set up an absolute barrier to change. For this reason, as well as because of its origins as a fusion of two conflicting social philosophies, it deserves the title "conservative liberalism."

According to the second, or "referee," version of pluralism, the role of the government is to oversee and regulate the competition among interest groups in the society. Out of the applications of this theory have grown not only countless laws, such as the antitrust bills, pure food and drug acts, and Taft-Hartley Law, but also the complex system of quasi-judicial regulatory agencies in the executive branch of government. Henry Kariel, in a powerful and convincing book entitled *The Decline of American Pluralism*, has shown that this referee function of government, as it actually works out in practice, systematically favors the interests of the stronger against the weaker party in interest-group conflicts and tends to solidify the power of those who already hold it. The government, therefore, plays a conservative, rather than a neutral, role in the society.

Kariel details the ways in which this discriminatory influence is exercised. In the field of regulation of labor unions, for example, the federal agencies deal with the established leadership of the unions. In such matters as the overseeing of union elections, the settlement of jurisdictional disputes, or the setting up of mediation boards, it is the interests of those leaders rather than the competing interests of rank-and-file dissidents which are favored. In the regulation of agriculture, again, the locally most influential farmers or leaders of farmers' organizations draw up the guidelines for control which are then adopted by the federal inspectors. In each case, ironically, the unwillingness of the government to impose its own standards or rules results not in a free play of competing groups, but in the enforcement of the preferences of the existing predominant interests.

In a sense, these unhappy consequences of government regulation stem from a confusion between a theory of interest-conflict and a theory of power-conflict. The government quite successfully referees the conflict among competing *powers*—any group which has already managed to accumulate a significant quantum of power will find its claims attended to by the federal agencies. But legitimate *interests* which have been ignored, suppressed, defeated, or which have not yet succeeded in organizing themselves for effective action, will find their disadvantageous position perpetuated through the decisions of the government. It is as though an umpire were to come upon a baseball game in progress between big boys and little boys, in which the

big boys cheated, broke the rules, claimed hits
that were outs, and made the little boys accept
the injustice by brute force. If the umpire undertakes to "regulate" the game by simply enforcing
the "rules" actually being practiced, he does not
thereby make the game a fair one. Indeed, he
may actually make matters worse, because if the
little boys get up their courage, band together,
and decide to fight it out, the umpire will accuse
them of breaking the rules and throw his weight
against them! Precisely the same sort of thing
happens in pluralist politics. For example, the
American Medical Association exercises a stran-
glehold over American medicine through its influence over the government's licensing regula-
tions. Doctors who are opposed to the A.M.A.'s
political positions, or even to its medical policies,
do not merely have to buck the entrenched authority of the organization's leaders. They must
also risk the loss of hospital affiliations, speciality
accreditation, and so forth, all of which powers
have been placed in the hands of the medical establishment by state and federal laws. Those laws
are written by the government in cooperation
with the very same A.M.A. leaders; not surpris-
ingly, the interests of dissenting doctors do not
receive favorable attention.

The net effect of government action is thus to
weaken, rather than strengthen, the play of conflicting interests in the society. The theory of
pluralism here has a crippling effect upon the
government, for it warns against positive federal
intervention in the name of independent principles of justice, equality, or fairness. The theory

says justice will emerge from the free interplay of opposed groups; the practice tends to destroy that interplay.

Finally, the theory of pluralism in all its forms has the effect in American thought and politics of discriminating not only against certain social groups or interests, but also against certain sorts of proposals for the solution of social problems. According to pluralist theory, politics is a contest among social groups for control of the power and decision of the government. Each group is motivated by some interest or cluster of interests and seeks to sway the government toward action in its favor. The typical social problem according to pluralism is therefore some instance of distributive injustice. One group is getting too much, another too little, of the available resources. In accord with its modification of traditional liberalism, pluralism's goal is a rough parity among competing groups rather than among competing individuals. Characteristically, new proposals originate with a group which feels that its legitimate interests have been slighted, and the legislative outcome is a measure which corrects the social imbalance to a degree commensurate with the size and political power of the initiating group.

But there are some social ills in America whose causes do not lie in a maldistribution of wealth, and which cannot be cured therefore by the techniques of pluralist politics. For example, America is growing uglier, more dangerous, and less pleasant to live in, as its citizens grow richer. The reason is that natural beauty, public order, the cultivation of the arts, are not the special interest of any identifiable social group. Consequently, evils and inadequacies in those areas cannot be remedied by shifting the distribution of wealth and power among existing social groups. To be sure, crime and urban slums hurt the poor more than the rich, the Negro more than the white—but fundamentally they are problems of the society as a whole, not of any particular group. That is to say, they concern the general good, not merely the aggregate of private goods. To deal with such problems, there must be some way of constituting the whole society a genuine group with a group purpose and a conception of the common good. Pluralism rules this out in theory by portraying society as an aggregate of human communities rather than as itself a human community; and it equally rules out a concern for the general good in practice by encouraging a politics of interest-group pressures in which there is no mechanism for the discovery and expression of the common good.

The theory and practice of pluralism first came to dominate American politics during the depression, when the Democratic party put together an electoral majority of minority groups. It is not at all surprising that the same period saw the demise of an active socialist movement. For socialism, both in its diagnosis of the ills of industrial capitalism and in its proposed remedies, focuses on the structure of the economy and society as a whole and advances programs in the name of the general good. Pluralism, both as theory and as practice, simply does not acknowledge the possibility of wholesale reorganization of the society. By insisting on the group nature of society, it denies the existence of society-wide interests—save the purely procedural interest in preserving the system of group pressures—and the possibility of communal action in pursuit of the general good.

A proof of this charge can be found in the commissions, committees, institutes, and conferences which are convened from time to time to ponder the "national interest." The membership of these assemblies always includes an enlightened business executive, a labor leader, an educator, several clergymen of various faiths, a woman, a literate general or admiral, and a few public figures of unquestioned sobriety and predictable views. The whole is a microcosm of the interest groups and hereditary groups which, according to pluralism, constitute American society. Any vision of the national interest which emerges from such a group will inevitably be a standard pluralist picture of a harmonious, cooperative, distributively just, *tolerant* America. One could hardly expect a committee of group representatives to decide that the pluralist system of social groups is an obstacle to the general good!

IV

Pluralist democracy, with its virtue, tolerance, constitutes the highest stage in the political development of industrial capitalism. It transcends the crude "limitations" of early individualistic liberalism and makes a place for the communitarian features of social life, as well as for the interest-group politics which emerged as a domesticated version of the class struggle. Pluralism is humane, benevolent, accommodating, and far more responsive to the evils of social injustice than either the egoistic liberalism or the traditionalistic conservatism from which it grew. But pluralism is fatally blind to the evils which afflict the entire body politic, and as a theory of society it obstructs consideration of precisely the sorts of thoroughgoing social revisions which may be needed to remedy those evils. Like all great social theories, pluralism answered a genuine social need during a significant period of history. Now, however, new problems confront America, problems not of distributive injustice but of the common good. We must give up the image of society as a battleground of competing groups and formulate an ideal of society more exalted than the mere acceptance of opposed interests and diverse customs. There is need for a new philosophy of community, beyond pluralism and beyond tolerance.

# TOLERANCE
# AND THE SCIENTIFIC OUTLOOK

BY BARRINGTON MOORE, JR.

Die Wahrheit ist so wenig bescheiden
als das Licht. . . . Bildet die Bescheidenheit
den Charakter der Untersuchung, so ist
sie eher ein Kennzeichen der Scheu vor
der Wahrheit als vor der Unwahrheit. *Sie
ist eine der Untersuchung vorgeschrie-
bene Angst, das Resultat zu finden*, ein
Präservativmittel vor der Wahrheit.

—KARL MARX

I did not foresee, not having the courage of my own thought: the growing
murderousness of the world. . . .

The best lack all conviction while the
  worst
Are full of passionate intensity.

—WILLIAM BUTLER YEATS

In this essay I shall try to argue a thesis that
once upon a time was taken for granted without
much thought about its justification and which

Presentation of an earlier version to a faculty seminar
at Columbia University, presided over by my good friend
Professor Otto Kirchheimer, disturbed my composure
and produced some revisions. I also wish to thank Har-
vard's Russian Research Center for material support.

nowadays seems a bit old-fashioned and naive. Very briefly it is that the secular and scientific outlook is adequate for both understanding and evaluating human affairs because it is able in principle, and less frequently in practice, to yield clear-cut answers to important questions. Properly used and understood, the secular and scientific outlook leads neither to flaccid acceptance of the world as it is, watery toleration of every doctrine because there might be some contribution somewhere, nor to the fanatical single-mindedness of the doctrinaire, willing that a thousand may perish in order that one shall be saved. Instead of paralyzing the will and the intellect the rational and secular outlook can nerve men for mortal combat when the situation calls for it and prevent them from fighting or simply being foolish when the situation calls for rational discussion or some other behavior. It can tell us when to be tolerant and when tolerance becomes intellectual cowardice and evasion.

To defend these large claims adequately is far beyond the capabilities of a short essay and very likely my own as well. In the first two parts of this essay I shall try to show that some of the more familiar intellectual objections do not necessarily hold. In the concluding section I will discuss certain political obstacles that seem much more serious.

Obviously a great deal depends on what one means by the scientific outlook. To begin with I should like to reject any intellectual approach to the problems of the modern world that takes the form of a veiled plea for a return to some variety of the traditional humanistic approach as something separate from and opposed to science. To pose the issue in terms of Sir Charles Snow's "two cultures" seems to me to miss the main point, since both technicist science and academic humanism seem to me fundamentally similar ways of dodging the big problems and encapsulating the intellect in a cocoon of professional esteem. The conception of science used here will be a broad one: whatever is established by sound reasoning and evidence may belong to science. Insights from literature and philosophy become part of science as they become established. Their gropings and explorations are part of the whole rational enterprise. Only when such thinkers refuse to submit themselves to verification do they separate themselves from science. For the essence of science, I would suggest, is simply the refusal to believe on the basis of hope.

Certain widespread notions about the supposed limitations of the secular and rational outlook (terms I shall use interchangeably with scientific) are part of the effort to grow such comforting cocoons and promote a form of pseudo-toleration common in scholarly debate, especially in Anglo-Saxon countries. One such alleged limitation is the proposition that objective knowledge about human affairs is at bottom an illusion and an impossibility. Two historians, a Marxist and a conservative, so the argument runs, can agree only on trivial and superficial facts, such as the dates when the Peloponnesian War began and ended. They cannot agree on the significant aspects of the war, the meaning and in-

terconnection of events, because their significance comes from the different and irreconcil-
able values with which the two historians begin
their task. To make the case more concrete let us
suppose that the Marxist attributes the origins of
the war to commercial rivalry between Athens
and Sparta, while the conservative in effect re-
plies "nonsense" and explains the outbreak in
terms of a series of diplomatic maneuvers and
countermaneuvers.

Now as a purely practical matter we may
agree at once that the task of reaching firm conclusions on even such questions as this one, where
passions do not run very high, is extraordinarily
difficult due to the inaccessibility of much of the
relevant evidence and to natural human limitations such as vanity and stubbornness. The one
generalization in social science that I have encountered, and which seems to me thoroughly
supported by the evidence, is the remark of a
vexed colleague: "No one ever convinces any-
body of anything." But the question at issue here
is one of principle and does not concern personal
limitations or those in the evidence. In regard to
the principle it is possible, indeed necessary, to
agree that all knowledge contains a subjective
component without accepting the conclusion
that agreement is impossible about important
questions.

A subjective component is a necessary in-
gredient in any knowledge because the number
of questions it is possible to ask about any seg-
ment of reality is quite literally infinite. Only a
few of them are worth answering. No classical

scholar in his right mind would seriously consider counting the number of dust spots on a modern text of Plato. Some sense of relevance to human needs and purposes is always part of any worthwhile search for truth. One need not agree with Oscar Wilde that the truth is seldom pure and never simple. But the notion of truth pure and simple is useless because it provides no way to distinguish significance from triviality.

The distinction between significant and trivial truth is nevertheless an objective one, independent of the whims and prejudices of any given investigator. Two criteria, it seems to me, necessarily govern all serious intellectual inquiry. One is simultaneously pragmatic and political. Men seek truths that will contribute to their own advantage in the contest with nature and other men. There is often a strong destructive component in this search. Let those who urge that "the truth" or "true" philosophy is always life-enhancing, in order to criticize the destructive consequences of modern physical science, recall that even Archimedes worked for the war industry of his day. This destructive component may or may not be unavoidable, a situation that varies from case to case. We must not allow it to disappear from sight simply because of alleged or even real benefits. One criterion for distinguishing significant from trivial truth is therefore the amount of benefit or harm that comes from its discovery.

By itself the pragmatic political criterion is inadequate, even for descriptive purposes. There is also an aesthetic criterion. The seeker after truth often searches for beauty, order, and symmetry in the area he has chosen to investigate, with no concern for further consequences. Today such a remark may seem a trifle naive. Any competent psychologist can show how the search for beauty and order arises from the most tabooed psychological origins; any competent historian can point to equally repulsive political and social consequences. Quite so. There is no need here to attack these propositions, which are in the main probably correct. They do not, however, contradict the main point, nor are they even relevant to it. The existence of an aesthetic criterion merely implies that aesthetic considerations are valid in distinguishing between trivial and significant truths.

In the evaluation of significant inquiry both criteria often occur. For example, there is some tendency to look down on forms of inquiry that have purely pragmatic-political ends, even if the end is the benefit of all humanity. Perhaps this attitude is partly a legacy of Greek aristocratic prejudice. Yet there are stronger reasons for sensing a trace of provincialism in such inquiry. How are we to know that our conceptions of what is good for humanity reflect more than the prejudices of our age and epoch? Hence we try to escape to a more universal realm of discourse, the one glimpsed for example in Plato's theory of Forms. Yet aesthetic criteria* of significance

---

* Aesthetic criteria, it should be plain, do not distinguish truth from falsehood. Many beautiful theories are wrong. And the scientific conception of beauty or aesthetic satisfaction is narrower than the artistic one.

too can become sterile and futile if pursued without regard for other concerns. Order, pattern, and symmetry can by themselves be quite trivial. I at any rate find little enlightenment in the fact that the behavior of motorists in obeying a traffic signal and statements of Catholic men about belief in the deity can both be plotted on a graph in such a way as to resemble one another as examples of conformance to and deviation from a norm in large groups of people.† The reasons for the similarity are sufficiently different to make the expression of similarity in mathematical terms seem no more than a *tour de force*. On the other hand, at the highest level of achievement, in the work of let us say a Darwin or a Pasteur, where the reasons for symmetry apply over a wide area in a genuinely novel way, both the pragmatic-political and the aesthetic criteria find a satisfactory reconciliation. So far social scientists have not yet produced equally imposing structures that have withstood the test of asking, "Is this theory true?"

Perhaps that is impossible in this area of inquiry. Without going into the problem further we may remark that the kinds of truth we seek in different fields of inquiry may show substantial variations and that one criterion may therefore be much more important than the other in different fields of knowledge.

It is important to recognize that both the prag-

† See F. H. Allport, "The J-Curve Hypothesis of Conforming Behavior," in T. M. Newcomb and E. L. Hartley, editors, *Readings in Social Psychology* (New York, 1947), 55-68.

matic-political and the aesthetic criteria are themselves subject to rational criticism and revision. Both have certainly changed in the course of history, though there is an important undercurrent of continuity and resemblance among different civilizations and intellectual traditions. There is also room in the scholarly and scientific enterprise for a wide variety of questions and answers, even within the same subject matter or discipline. But to the extent that the answers are correct, they are compatible and congruent.

The Marxist interpretation of the Peloponnesian War will be very different from one written by a traditional diplomatic historian. As long as neither historian makes a mistake or suppresses relevant evidence, the accounts do not contradict but supplement each other. There are at the same time likely to be features of the interpretation that do conflict. These have to be settled by appeal to evidence. The old-fashioned diplomatic historian might point out that Sparta was a self-contained agrarian society and that even in Athens commercial activities played a secondary role. If he demonstrated these points with satisfactory reasoning and factual evidence, he would succeed in proving that the Marxist was just plain wrong. Tolerance for different "interpretations" based on different *Weltanschauungen* merely befuddles the issue.

All this amounts to the position that social reality past and present has a structure and meaning of its own that the scholar discovers in the same way an explorer discovers an ocean or a lake. The structure is there to begin with. The-

A man in search of
a woman — extraordinaire
of childbearing age
to love & care for.

ories help us to see it and prevent us from seeing it. They do not create the structure. Notions
about the constitutive role of reason seem to me
to be one source of the befuddlement here. Another is confusion between the meanings of objective and non-partisan. In the social sciences
and history, significant facts are bound to be
partisan in the sense that they upset *somebody's*
cherished pre-conceptions. There is a greater
likelihood that the truth will be subversive of the
established order than the other way around simply because all establishments have a vested interest in hiding some of the sources of their privileged position. But this is no more than a prob-
ability. There is no guarantee whatever that a
critical conception of society is a correct one.
The honest investigator has to be prepared for
the possibility that his findings and political pre-
conceptions fail to match. That few of us succeed in facing such discrepancies is painfully
obvious.

Certain further conclusions about the role of
tolerance in serious intellectual discussions and
scholarly research derive from this position.
While we may accept some of the modern scholar's self-imposed limitations as at times due to
the magnitude of the task and the frailty of the
flesh, we cannot out of charity erect these limitations into general principles of research. And
there are good grounds for caution in dispens-
ing even this form of charity. Very often a problem looks overwhelmingly complicated because
the simple answer that will organize the details
carries with it implications that are disagreeable

to the investigator for other reasons. Facts can and have been used to conceal the truth as well as to reveal it. Marx's warning about the real meaning of intellectual modesty, chosen as the epigraph for this essay, probably cannot be used as a universal epistemological principle. Yet it is a good working rule to be on the lookout for this possibility.

It would be an error to construe these observations as a general sneer at the specialist. There are specialists and specialists. The burden of the argument so far has been that such notions as "important," "interesting," "significant," "futile," and "trivial" have a strong objective component. They are not merely epithets that reflect the subjective whims of an individual critic, even though the words would make no sense if there were no human beings in the world to whose aspirations and problems the terms refer. Obviously the work of the specialist, when it sheds light on a significant problem, is in itself significant. Such a conception merely helps to distinguish between the indispensable specialization necessary to advances in knowledge and that which arises out of careerist concerns, intellectual fads, or sheer lack of talent. Similarly it should be obvious that objective standards apply to the work of synthesis and general explanation. The dilettante who has "perceptive" but incorrect notions about a hodgepodge of books deserves as much condemnation as the narrow technician creeping up some ladder of promotion by keeping his mouth shut on every issue that matters. Indeed the dilettante deserves greater condemnation because the technician can under appropriate circumstances help to establish worthwhile knowledge. When pseudo-brilliance sheds light, that is purely an accident.

On the other hand, it is absolutely necessary to keep the door open for the chance of a favorable accident, and, much more important, for those truths endeavoring to gain acceptance in the teeth of established orthodoxies. According to the scientific outlook, every idea, including the most dangerous and apparently absurd ones, deserves to have its credentials examined. Still, examining credentials means exactly that. It does not mean accepting the idea. Toleration implies the existence of a distinctive procedure for testing ideas, resembling due process in the realm of law. No one holds that under due process every accused person must be acquitted. A growing and changing procedure for the testing of ideas lies at the heart of any conception of tolerance tied to the scientific outlook. That is genuine tolerance. It has nothing to do with a cacophony of screaming fakers marketing political nostrums in the public square. Nor does the real article exist where various nuances of orthodoxy pass for academic freedom.

## II

In the area of serious political concerns, the scientific outlook seems to many thoughtful people today to have demonstrated its ultimate futility and failure. Explanations of political behavior remain feasible within this framework, some of its critics might concede. Rational criticism, on the other hand, appears impossible, except at the technical level of asserting that certain means are unlikely to bring about the desired results, i.e., concentration camps may not be the most efficient way to eliminate the Jews. If the purpose of the state is eliminating Jews, there is nothing more to be said from this conception of a scientific standpoint. The goals of the state are for the political scientist brute facts to be entered in his calculations the way a physicist enters gravity, friction, and the character of metals in his computations. According to this viewpoint, the moment the political scientist steps out of his professional role to assert that killing Jews is morally bad, he enters the realm of "values," loses his aura of professional competence, and becomes no more qualified to give authoritative guidance than any of the rest of us. For one set of "values" is supposedly as valid as any other.

Such seems to have been the outcome of the spirit of rational and scientific inquiry into political affairs. To at least a minority of contemporary thinkers the result seems both paradoxical and monstrous. Detachment and tolerance seem to have run riot and turned upside down. There has been a variety of attempts to escape from the paradox and restore to rational criticism the legitimacy that seemed to vanish with the decline of religion and metaphysics.

Most of these involve in some degree a surrender of rationality and a return to religious or quasi-religious conceptions. Even neo-Marxist or secular Hegelian efforts do not seem to me altogether free of this surrender. In all these efforts the fundamental feature is an attempt to derive a notion of purpose for human life and society by connecting it somehow with the structure of history or the universe. Even if we could agree on the existence of certain historical trends, such as ever-increasing control over the physical world, this fact in and by itself carries no obligation that we should approve it or disapprove it, fight for it or against it. The attempt to derive legitimacy for any set of values from some source external to living humans—and history is external insofar as the past confronts us with a world we never made—seems to me both doomed to frustration and unnecessary.

It is doomed to frustration because no alternative to rationality, no call to faith no matter how disguised, can in the end withstand the corrosive effects of rational inquiry. This is true even if the secular outlook suffers a more than partial eclipse for many long years to come. Furthermore is it not time to throw away the metaphysical crutch and walk on our own two legs? Rather than attempt to revive a dubious ontology and epistemology I would urge that we recognize that God and his metaphysical surrogates are dead, and learn to take the consequences.

If men wish to make others suffer or even to destroy civilization itself, there is nothing outside of man himself to which one can appeal in order to assert that such actions deserve condemnation. Hence the problem of evaluation, like that of objective knowledge, becomes one of trying to discover if there are some aspects of what is loosely called the human situation that might provide a suitable point from which to argue. Again, as in the case of knowledge, it is a problem of trying to demonstrate that the introduction of a subjective component does not lead to purely arbitrary results.

In conversation about values one frequently encounters people who will assert for the sake of argument that they want to make human beings suffer. It is difficult to know whether one should take this argument seriously. As far as I am aware, no human group has ever seriously held that pain and suffering were desirable in themselves. That they have been regarded as a means to an end in many cultures is of course obvious. On the other hand, it is clear that there is pleasure to be had in making people suffer, indeed in watching them suffer. Hence we will do well to take the argument seriously.

There seem to be only two observations to make in reply to such an argument. The first is that if one is serious, one must be prepared to take the consequences. The second is that the consequences if pushed very far are likely to be the disintegration of human society, including that sector to which the believer in cruelty belongs. Those who do believe at all seriously in cruelty usually exclude the victims from "real" humanity. As a supreme value cruelty is probably incompatible with the continued existence of humanity. The fact that large amounts of cruelty are perfectly compatible with the continued existence of human society does not necessarily affect this thesis. Such cruelty is generally instrumental, and not an end in itself.

Even if this argument were watertight, it would not be very satisfactory. It tells us very little about the huge masses of cruelty that are everywhere around us, and to which we would like to find a reasoned objection. Perhaps it will be possible to make better progress by taking a concrete example, that of Nazi Germany. What would be a tenable argument that constituted an indictment of Hitlerite Germany?

One reply, for which I have considerable respect, asserts in effect that the mere search for some ground on which to base the indictment constitutes a survival of the religious and metaphysical outlook. Hence the query is foolish. One has to take a stand for or against Nazism and, accepting the consequences, fight to establish the ultimate premises of society. This seems to be the core of the existentialist position. Born into a world we did not make, there is no possibility of escaping this terrible ambiguity.

But is the situation as ambiguous as all that? There are grounds for holding that it is not and that warrants for judgment can be derived from certain factual aspects of human existence. If we are to live at all, we have to live in society. And if we are to live in society it may as well be with as little pain as possible.* The suffering that is

---

*Against the notion that a minimum of suffering might provide a sound criterion for evaluating forms of society, there is the objection that varieties of suffering and happiness are incommensurable. To a sociologist the objection carries little weight. Certainly there are enormous

unavoidable will differ under differing circumstances and certainly is not the same at all stages of history. To establish what this minimum may be is no easy task. The general intellectual procedures, to be specified in a moment, are reasonably clear and well known. They seem to me to deserve the label "scientific."

If an unambiguous starting point is to be found, it is through the analysis of the prerequisites of human existence along the lines just suggested. In other words, values are human demands put upon the human environment. To establish them is no task to be performed once and for all. It changes with changing historical conditions. This much of the existentialist stress on permanent ambiguity has a firm foundation. But if we return to the Nazi case and certain types of criticism, mainly Marxist, that actually have been made of this society, it may be possible to discern the constant and recurring features of rational social criticism. My intention here is

---

varieties of each. Yet it is not too difficult to determine when the happiness of some people depends on the misery of others. The criterion of minimal suffering implies that such situations ought to be changed when it is possible to do so. This possibility may not exist. The notion that freely accepted rational authority constitutes freedom and happiness is absurd as a universal generalization. Accepted burdens are still burdens. A much more serious difficulty arises from the introduction of the time element. How much should present generations suffer for the sake of those to come? How much of the horrors of the industrial revolution and of the construction of socialism in Russia are justifiable from this standpoint? I try to discuss these difficulties in the final section.

not to consider specific factual theses about National Socialist Germany but rather to exhibit very briefly the characteristic structure of a certain type of argument.

First, there is the premise, whose basis has just been discussed, to the effect that unnecessary suffering produced by an historically specific form of government or society is bad and that the social order ought to be changed. To demonstrate the existence of this suffering and its historical causes is the most important and in practice the most difficult part of the argument. Secondly, it is necessary, and indeed part of the same task, to break the illusion that the present is inevitable and permanent. Showing its historical roots performs part of this task. Demonstrating who gains and who suffers, and what concrete interests are at work to preserve the prevailing system are also part of this task. Finally, and this is often more difficult, it is necessary to show that good grounds exist for holding that the society could be arranged in such a way as to produce less suffering. In the case of Nazi Germany it would be necessary, for example, to show that unemployment could have been eliminated in other ways than by a program of armaments and foreign conquest. Essentially the procedure amounts to demonstrating that existing social facts contain the potentiality of becoming something different from what they are.

This is more or less the common working procedure of a number of social scientists, though perhaps only a minority. The last point about demonstrating the potentiality of less suffering may seem to some Hegelians to require intellectual procedures fundamentally different from those of secular science as conceived here. I do not think that this is so. Potentiality is as much an empirical fact as any other and has to be discovered in the same way. To show that German society could work with less suffering, one would have to discuss the high level of technology, education, and similar factors, as well as the forces opposing change. The conclusion might well be that only military defeat could change the situation. Now it is true that this could never be proved, any more than one could prove that capitalism or socialism would work, before they had been tried. Some thinkers seize on this point to argue that social science is qualitatively different from other forms of rational thought. Does it come to any more than the fact that experiment is impossible in such matters? The potentiality of new chemical forms out of old is demonstrable by experiment, that of new social forms out of old perhaps fortunately remains impossible.

If the argument up to this point is correct, there are no absolute barriers to objective knowledge and objective evaluation of human institutions. Objective here means simply that correct and unambiguous answers, independent of individual whims and preferences, are in principle possible. A real distinction exists, in other words, between scientific humility and the vagueness that comes from moral and intellectual cowardice. There are situations, to be discussed shortly, where judiciousness becomes the last refuge of the scoundrel.

### III

Barriers there are to the use of rational thought, even if they are not necessarily located in the realm of philosophy. They are formidable enough and could well overwhelm it.

The possibility of debating political issues in a rational manner arises only in some version of a free society. So much is this the case that we are inclined today to measure the extent of freedom in a society by the amount of public controversy that exists. Though this conception is inadequate by itself because it ignores the character of the issues in the debate and the quality of its conduct, it does draw attention to an important part of the truth. One crucial characteristic of a free society is the absence of a single overriding "national purpose." The attempts, never completely successful, to impose such a purpose are the stigma of the modern totalitarian state.

Within very broad limits diversity of taste and opinion is a positive good in its own right, according to the democratic creed, and not merely a means to an end. Without this diversity human beings cannot hope to develop their varying qualities. The usual limitation posed is that in cultivating such tastes they must not injure others. There are difficulties in this conception: how does one distinguish real injury from outraged prejudice? The hints given in the preceding section must suffice to suggest that the problem is not altogether insoluble. At any rate a society with the maximum amount of freedom possible could not allow its members to gratify every whim and impulse: to kill a parent, child, spouse, or colleague in a fit of exasperation has to be tabu. Even so a free society, as democratic theorists to a great extent recognize, requires rather extraordinary people to make it run. Its members must be remarkably intelligent and well-informed, as well as sufficiently self-restrained to be able to give way in a passionate argument that goes against their interests.

These remarks suffice to recall the main features and some of the problems of the democratic political model. The place of tolerance and rationality are sufficiently familiar to enable us to dispense with any special discussion of them. The real problems lie elsewhere. How realistic is the democratic model, especially in the second half of the twentieth century amid conditions of revolutionary and international conflict? If it is unrealistic, what are we to do with the ideal of free and rational discussion? Shall we be "realistic" and junk it in our actual practices, while saving it to decorate those increasingly solemn occasions when we reaffirm our national solidarity in times of crisis? By and large this seems to be the direction in which events are moving in the West. Still it remains possible to find at least a small public audience for highly critical notions as long as the critic constitutes no obstacle to "serious" policy. If the situation becomes more tense it may be necessary to get rid of the critics. Rough methods may not be needed. Much of what passes for criticism turns out on examination to be a different note in the chorus of praise for western "freedom," and for the acceptance of the Cold War and the destructive civilization dependent on it. Those who accuse the pacifists of merely trying to opt out of the struggle are, I believe, largely correct. With a few distinguished exceptions those who try to frighten us with the horrors of war avoid analyzing the social and political costs of peace, which might well be catastrophic. Can the scientific outlook tell us anything about the prospects for tolerant rational discussion, or the conditions under which it may be out of place? It is my contention here that it can.

Among the conditions that make possible improvement within the prevailing political system are these. First and foremost there has to be a substantial group of people with a material interest in change. On the other side, the rich and powerful have to be able and willing to make concessions. Three sets of factors are significant in this connection. The upper classes have to possess a sufficient economic margin to feel that the concessions will not crucially damage its position. The emergence of new sources of wealth can be important in this connection. Secondly, the existence of diverse interests among the upper classes, all of them more or less flourishing, helps to prevent the formation of a solid block of privilege against the claims of the lower classes. Finally, the existence of political institutions, such as a parliament and a judiciary with traditional roots in the past and yet workable with new men and new problems, helps the functioning of an open society. This complex of conditions was present during the transition to modern industrial society in England; they were absent in Germany and Russia.

These conditions themselves, however, were the consequence of revolution. All the major democracies, England, France, and the United States passed through a period of civil war or revolutionary violence (the difference is mainly one of terminology) which by destroying or crippling certain features of the old order—royal absolutism in England, the landed aristocracy in France, plantation slavery in the United States— made possible long periods of social struggle within the democratic framework.

Revolutionary violence, including dictatorship, has been the precursor of periods of extended freedom at several points in western history. It is simply impossible to put violence, dictatorship, and fanaticism in one category; freedom, constitutionalism, and civil liberties in another. The first has played a part in the development of the second. To deny the connection is no more than a partisan trick. It becomes a hollow partisan trick when in the name of democracy one condones saturation bombing against peasant revolutionaries; hollower still if one chooses to condone such violence and then criticize a Robespierre for shedding blood in the name of future liberty.* Liberal rhetoric can be

* The argument connecting terrorism with a specific philosophy of history may be mainly myth. There is a good deal of evidence to show that Robespierre was a political trimmer; furthermore, that the main victims of revolutionary terror were in plain fact enemies of the revolution. We associate Stalin, correctly in my view,

as full of nauseating hypocrisy as any other. Even so, it is a disastrous error to junk the whole of liberalism. There are grounds in historical experience for the liberal suspicion of those who preach some version of the doctrine that the historical end justifies present blood-letting—usually somebody else's blood too. Our shudder at violence, when we still have these shudders, is not just bourgeois prejudice. Hence it is worthwhile trying to specify some of the conditions under which the resort to violence is justified in the name of freedom.

Three main considerations may be advanced to justify the refusal to work within the prevailing system and the adoption of a revolutionary attitude. One is that the prevailing regime is unnecessarily repressive, i.e., that the essential work of society could continue with less suffering and constraint. The upholders of the prevailing order will almost certainly define the essential tasks of society differently from its opponents. To find some basis for a rational decision on this point is far from easy if one insists on logical rigor. Nevertheless, as pointed out before, negative evaluations are considerably easier to reach. Whatever positive values we commit ourselves to, in addition to freedom, we do not want cruelty, injustice, waste and misuse of resources for destructive purposes. Secondly, there has to be substantial evidence that a revolutionary situa-

with some of the worst terrors in human history. But he treated Marxist theory contemptuously when it suited his purpose. The whole question deserves fresh and skeptical scrutiny.

tion is ripening. Ripeness means not only that the destructive aspects of the revolution will enjoy enough support to carry them out, but, more importantly, that there are realistic prospects for introducing a better system: that the level of potential economic production is high enough to permit a more rational organization and also that the human skills are available (or will be shortly) in order to operate the whole society with less pain, suffering, and self-generated stupidity. Finally, there has to be a rough calculus of revolutionary violence. Before the resort to revolution is justifiable, there has to be good reason to believe that the costs in human suffering and degradation inherent in the continuation of the status quo really outweigh those to be incurred in the revolution and its aftermath. To put the point with appalling crudeness, one has to weigh the casualties of a reign of terror against those of allowing the prevailing situation to continue, which may include a high death rate due to disease, ignorance—or at the other end of the scale, failure to control the use of powerful technical devices. (The 40,000 deaths a year in the United States due to automobile accidents come to mind here. What would we think of a political regime that executed 40,000 people a year?)

Miscalculation on all of these points constitutes one of the main reasons for the horrors of the Bolshevik Revolution and the Stalinist era. The miscalculation is the more significant because many of the forerunners and leaders of Russian Marxism were keenly aware of the issues posed here and debated them hotly among themselves. Does the fate of the Bolshevik Revolution then indicate the futility of raising the issues and considerations discussed here? Is there not something presumptuous and silly in the attempt to pass judgment on revolutions? Passing judgment in the form of apologetics for the *ancien régime* or for its revolutionary successor (an exercise which constitutes the bulk of run-of-the-mill history) does seem futile. On the other hand, the attempt to discover what might have been rational, in the sense of obtaining the maximum result with a minimum of suffering, is not wholly a waste of time. Hypotheses about present and future events are not like the hypotheses of the historian. By making such hypotheses, important historical actors also contribute, within limits, to the shaping of events. These limits vary from situation to situation. But there seems to be an inherent principle of ambiguity in the flow of human affairs, a point that Merleau-Ponty has argued at great length. The implication increases the burden of responsibility on anyone who chooses to step outside the current framework of peaceful debate to advocate an extreme course. Even if the revolutionary course succeeds, one can never be sure that it was absolutely necessary. On the other side too, endless Hamlet-like waiting for fuller information and exactly the right moment may mean letting the crucial moment pass by default. Ultimately there is no avoiding this frightening dilemma. Perhaps there is an encouraging aspect to the fact that human beings are endowed with a strong dose of irrational passion. Otherwise all our struggles would have come to naught, and we would still be in the Stone Age.

Fortunately the task of the professional intellectual, with whom we are mainly concerned in this essay, is in some respects easier than that of the political leader. The real task of the intellectual is *not* to be committed to any political doctrine or ideal, *not* to be an agitator or a fighter, but to find and speak the truth, whatever the political consequences may be. Even if, as we have said, political concerns help to determine what truths intellectuals look for, the truths they uncover may often be and actually are extremely damaging to exactly these concerns. To be more concrete and immediate, if the intellectual finds that the current situation is one of sham debate and unnecessary repression, yet without any serious prospect for change, he has the task of relentless, critical exposure—destructive criticism of a destructive reality. His commitment to politically significant truth carries with it the obligation to point out the illusions, equivocations, ambiguities, and hypocrisies of those who raise the banner of freedom in order to perpetuate brutality, be they Communist or anti-Communist.

*Tout comprendre c'est tout pardonner* is one of those catchy phrases that often enough turn out to be sloppy half-truths. For a clear understanding of how any society really works is likely to be the first step toward condemnation because it enables men to see not only the seamy side, to penetrate behind the glorifications and equivocations, but also to realize possibilities for im-

provement. The notion that a scientific attitude
toward human society necessarily induces a
conservative tolerance of the existing order, or
that it deprives thinkers of insight into the important issues of the past and the present seems
to me totally absurd. These things do happen
and on a very wide scale, but constitute a failure
to live up to the requirements and implications of
the scientific outlook.

To this one might object that the attitude
toward science advocated here is like that of the
Mahometan toward the Koran: since what is
not in the Koran is not true and not necessary for
salvation, and since the Koran contains every-
thing valuable in other books, the rest may be
cast on the flames. To the extent that the conception of science suggested here is a very broad
one, the comparison holds. The thrust of the argument has been that the necessity for a subjective element in understanding and evaluating
human affairs does not automatically introduce
an irreducible arbitrary element into such judgments, difficult though it may be to eliminate this
element for other reasons. Still the comparison is
false for one crucial reason. Unlike the Koran,
no part of science, no conception of science and
its methods, and least of all the present one, is
permanently above and beyond investigation,
criticism, and if need be, fundamental change.
Science is tolerant of reason; relentlessly intolerant of unreason and sham. A flickering light in
our darkness it is, as Morris Cohen once said, but
the only one we have, and woe to him who
would put it out.

# REPRESSIVE TOLERANCE

BY HERBERT MARCUSE

THIS essay examines the idea of tolerance in our advanced industrial society. The conclusion reached is that the realization of the objective of tolerance would call for intolerance toward prevailing policies, attitudes, opinions, and the extension of tolerance to policies, attitudes, and opinions which are outlawed or suppressed. In other words, today tolerance appears again as what it was in its origins, at the beginning of the modern period—a partisan goal, a subversive liberating notion and practice. Conversely, what is proclaimed and practiced as tolerance today, is in many of its most effective manifestations serving the cause of oppression.

The author is fully aware that, at present, no power, no authority, no government exists which would translate liberating tolerance into practice, but he believes that it is the task and duty of the intellectual to recall and preserve historical possibilities which seem to have become utopian possibilities—that it is his task to break the concreteness of oppression in order to open the men-

This essay is dedicated to my students at Brandeis University.

tal space in which this society can be recognized as what it is and does.

Tolerance is an end in itself. The elimination of violence, and the reduction of suppression to the extent required for protecting man and animals from cruelty and aggression are preconditions for the creation of a humane society. Such a society does not yet exist; progress toward it is perhaps more than before arrested by violence and suppression on a global scale. As deterrents against nuclear war, as police action against subversion, as technical aid in the fight against imperialism and communism, as methods of pacification in neo-colonial massacres, violence and suppression are promulgated, practiced, and defended by democratic and authoritarian governments alike, and the people subjected to these governments are educated to sustain such practices as necessary for the preservation of the status quo. Tolerance is extended to policies, conditions, and modes of behavior which should not be tolerated because they are impeding, if not destroying, the chances of creating an existence without fear and misery.

This sort of tolerance strengthens the tyranny of the majority against which authentic liberals protested. The political locus of tolerance has changed: while it is more or less quietly and constitutionally withdrawn from the opposition, it is made compulsory behavior with respect to established policies. Tolerance is turned from an active into a passive state, from practice to non-practice: laissez-faire the constituted authorities.

It is the people who tolerate the government, which in turn tolerates opposition within the framework determined by the constituted authorities.

Tolerance toward that which is radically evil now appears as good because it serves the cohesion of the whole on the road to affluence or more affluence. The toleration of the systematic moronization of children and adults alike by publicity and propaganda, the release of destructiveness in aggressive driving, the recruitment for and training of special forces, the impotent and benevolent tolerance toward outright deception in merchandising, waste, and planned obsolescence are not distortions and aberrations, they are the essence of a system which fosters tolerance as a means for perpetuating the struggle for existence and suppressing the alternatives. The authorities in education, morals, and psychology are vociferous against the increase in juvenile delinquency; they are less vociferous against the proud presentation, in word and deed and pictures, of ever more powerful missiles, rockets, bombs——the mature delinquency of a whole civilization.

According to a dialectical proposition it is the whole which determines the truth—not in the sense that the whole is prior or superior to its parts, but in the sense that its structure and function determine every particular condition and relation. Thus, within a repressive society, even progressive movements threaten to turn into their opposite to the degree to which they accept the rules of the game. To take a most controversial case: the exercise of political rights (such as voting, letter-writing to the press, to Senators, etc., protest-demonstrations with a priori renunciation of counterviolence) in a society of total administration serves to strengthen this administration by testifying to the existence of democratic liberties which, in reality, have changed their content and lost their effectiveness. In such a case, freedom (of opinion, of assembly, of speech) becomes an instrument for absolving servitude. And yet (and only here the dialectical proposition shows its full intent) the existence and practice of these liberties remain a precondition for the restoration of their original oppositional function, provided that the effort to transcend their (often self-imposed) limitations is intensified. Generally, the function and value of tolerance depend on the equality prevalent in the society in which tolerance is practiced. Tolerance itself stands subject to overriding criteria: its range and its limits cannot be defined in terms of the respective society. In other words, tolerance is an end in itself only when it is truly universal, practiced by the rulers as well as by the ruled, by the lords as well as by the peasants, by the sheriffs as well as by their victims. And such universal tolerance is possible only when no real or alleged enemy requires in the national interest the education and training of people in military violence and destruction. As long as these conditions do not prevail, the conditions of tolerance are "loaded": they are determined and defined by the institutionalized inequality (which is certainly compatible with

constitutional equality), i.e., by the class structure of society. In such a society, tolerance is
*de facto* limited on the dual ground of legalized
violence or suppression (police, armed forces,
guards of all sorts) and of the privileged position
held by the predominant interests and their "con-
nections."

These background limitations of tolerance are
normally prior to the explicit and judicial limitations as defined by the courts, custom, governments, etc. (for example, "clear and present
danger," threat to national security, heresy).
Within the framework of such a social structure,
tolerance can be safely practiced and proclaimed.
It is of two kinds: (1) the passive toleration of
entrenched and established attitudes and ideas
even if their damaging effect on man and nature
is evident; and (2) the active, official tolerance
granted to the Right as well as to the Left, to
movements of aggression as well as to movements
of peace, to the party of hate as well as to that of
humanity. I call this non-partisan tolerance "abstract" or "pure" inasmuch as it refrains from
taking sides—but in doing so it actually protects
the already established machinery of discrimination.

The tolerance which enlarged the range and
content of freedom was always partisan—intolerant toward the protagonists of the repressive
status quo. The issue was only the degree and
extent of intolerance. In the firmly established
liberal society of England and the United States,
freedom of speech and assembly was granted
even to the radical enemies of society, provided

they did not make the transition from word to deed, from speech to action.

Relying on the effective background limitations imposed by its class structure, the society seemed to practice general tolerance. But liberalist theory had already placed an important condition on tolerance: it was "to apply only to human beings in the maturity of their faculties." John Stuart Mill does not only speak of children and minors; he elaborates: "Liberty, as a principle, has no application to any state of things anterior to the time when mankind have become capable of being improved by free and equal discussion." Anterior to that time, men may still be barbarians, and "despotism is a legitimate mode of government in dealing with barbarians, provided the end be their improvement, and the means justified by actually effecting that end." Mill's often-quoted words have a less familiar implication on which their meaning depends: the internal connection between liberty and truth. There is a sense in which truth is the end of liberty, and liberty must be defined and confined by truth. Now in what sense can liberty be for the sake of truth? Liberty is self-determination, autonomy—this is almost a tautology, but a tautology which results from a whole series of synthetic judgments. It stipulates the ability to determine one's own life: to be able to determine what to do and what not to do, what to suffer and what not. But the subject of this autonomy is never the contingent, private individual as that which he actually is or happens to be;

it is rather the individual as a human being who is capable of being free with the others. And the problem of making possible such a harmony between every individual liberty and the other is not that of finding a compromise between competitors, or between freedom and law, between general and individual interest, common and private welfare in an *established* society, but of *creating* the society in which man is no longer enslaved by institutions which vitiate self-determination from the beginning. In other words, freedom is still to be created even for the freest of the existing societies. And the direction in which it must be sought, and the institutional and cultural changes which may help to attain the goal are, at least in developed civilization, *comprehensible*, that is to say, they can be identified and projected, on the basis of experience, by human reason.

In the interplay of theory and practice, true and false solutions become distinguishable—never with the evidence of necessity, never as the positive, only with the certainty of a reasoned and reasonable chance, and with the persuasive force of the negative. For the true positive is the society of the future and therefore beyond definition and determination, while the existing positive is that which must be surmounted. But the experience and understanding of the existent society may well be capable of identifying what is *not* conducive to a free and rational society, what impedes and distorts the possibilities of its creation. Freedom is liberation, a specific historical process in theory and practice, and as such it has its right and wrong, its truth and falsehood.

The uncertainty of chance in this distinction does not cancel the historical objectivity, but it necessitates freedom of thought and expression as preconditions of finding the way to freedom— it necessitates *tolerance*. However, this tolerance cannot be indiscriminate and equal with respect to the contents of expression, neither in word nor in deed; it cannot protect false words and wrong deeds which demonstrate that they contradict and counteract the possibilities of liberation. Such indiscriminate tolerance is justified in harmless debates, in conversation, in academic discussion; it is indispensable in the scientific enterprise, in private religion. But society cannot be indiscriminate where the pacification of existence, where freedom and happiness themselves are at stake: here, certain things cannot be said, certain ideas cannot be expressed, certain policies cannot be proposed, certain behavior cannot be permitted without making tolerance an instrument for the continuation of servitude.

The danger of "destructive tolerance" (Baudelaire), of "benevolent neutrality" toward *art* has been recognized: the market, which absorbs equally well (although with often quite sudden fluctuations) art, anti-art, and non-art, all possible conflicting styles, schools, forms, provides a "complacent receptacle, a friendly abyss" (Edgar Wind, *Art and Anarchy* (New York: Knopf, 1964), p. 101) in which the radical impact of art, the protest of art against the estab-

lished reality is swallowed up. However, censorship of art and literature is regressive under all
circumstances. The authentic oeuvre is not and
cannot be a prop of oppression, and pseudo-art
(which can be such a prop) is not art. Art stands
against history, withstands history which has
been the history of oppression, for art subjects
reality to laws other than the established ones: to
the laws of the Form which creates a different
reality—negation of the established one even
where art depicts the established reality. But in
its struggle with history, art subjects itself to
history: history enters the definition of art and
enters into the distinction between art and
pseudo-art. Thus it happens that what was once
art becomes pseudo-art. Previous forms, styles,
and qualities, previous modes of protest and refusal cannot be recaptured in or against a different society. There are cases where an authentic
oeuvre carries a regressive political message—
Dostoevski is a case in point. But then, the message is canceled by the oeuvre itself: the regressive political content is absorbed, *aufgehoben* in
the artistic form: in the work as literature.

Tolerance of free speech is the way of improvement, of progress in liberation, *not* because
there is no objective truth, and improvement
must necessarily be a compromise between a
variety of opinions, but because there *is* an objective truth which can be discovered, ascer-
tained only in learning and comprehending that
which is and that which can be and ought to be
done for the sake of improving the lot of mankind. This common and historical "ought" is not

immediately evident, at hand: it has to be un-
covered by "cutting through," "splitting,"
"breaking asunder" (*dis-cutio*) the given material—separating right and wrong, good and bad,
correct and incorrect. The subject whose "improvement" depends on a progressive historical
practice is each man as man, and this universality
is reflected in that of the discussion, which a
priori does not exclude any group or individual.
But even the all-inclusive character of liberalist
tolerance was, at least in theory, based on the
proposition that men were (potential) *individuals* who could learn to hear and see and feel by
themselves, to develop their own thoughts, to
grasp their true interests and rights and capabilities, also against established authority and opinion. This was the rationale of free speech and assembly. Universal toleration becomes question-
able when its rationale no longer prevails, when
tolerance is administered to manipulated and indoctrinated individuals who parrot, as their own,
the opinion of their masters, for whom heterono-
my has become autonomy.

The telos of tolerance is truth. It is clear from
the historical record that the authentic spokesmen of tolerance had more and other truth in
mind than that of propositional logic and academic theory. John Stuart Mill speaks of the
truth which is persecuted in history and which
does *not* triumph over persecution by virtue of
its "inherent power," which in fact has no inherent power "against the dungeon and the stake."
And he enumerates the "truths" which were
cruelly and successfully liquidated in the dun-

geons and at the stake: that of Arnold of Brescia, of Fra Dolcino, of Savonarola, of the Albigensians, Waldensians, Lollards, and Hussites. Tolerance is first and foremost for the sake of the heretics—the historical road toward *humanitas* appears as heresy: target of persecution by the powers that be. Heresy by itself, however, is no token of truth.

The criterion of progress in freedom according to which Mill judges these movements is the Reformation. The evaluation is *ex post,* and his list includes opposites (Savonarola too would have burned Fra Dolcino). Even the ex post evaluation is contestable as to its truth: history corrects the judgment—too late. The correction does not help the victims and does not absolve their executioners. However, the lesson is clear: intolerance has delayed progress and has prolonged the slaughter and torture of innocents for hundreds of years. Does this clinch the case for indiscriminate, "pure" tolerance? Are there historical conditions in which such toleration impedes liberation and multiplies the victims who are sacrificed to the status quo? Can the indiscriminate guaranty of political rights and liberties be repressive? Can such tolerance serve to contain qualitative social change?

I shall discuss this question only with reference to political movements, attitudes, schools of thought, philosophies which are "political" in the widest sense—affecting the society as a whole, demonstrably transcending the sphere of privacy. Moreover, I propose a shift in the focus of the discussion: it will be concerned not only, and not primarily, with tolerance toward radical extremes, minorities, subversives, etc., but rather with tolerance toward majorities, toward official and public opinion, toward the established protectors of freedom. In this case, the discussion can have as a frame of reference only a democratic society, in which the people, as individuals and as members of political and other organizations, participate in the making, sustaining, and changing policies. In an authoritarian system, the people do not tolerate—they suffer established policies.

Under a system of constitutionally guaranteed and (generally and without too many and too glaring exceptions) practiced civil rights and liberties, opposition and dissent are tolerated unless they issue in violence and/or in exhortation to and organization of violent subversion. The underlying assumption is that the established society is free, and that any improvement, even a change in the social structure and social values, would come about in the normal course of events, prepared, defined, and tested in free and equal discussion, on the open marketplace of ideas and goods.* Now in recalling John Stuart

* I wish to reiterate for the following discussion that, *de facto*, tolerance is *not* indiscriminate and "pure" even in the most democratic society. The "background limitations" stated on page 85 restrict tolerance before it begins to operate. The antagonistic structure of society rigs the rules of the game. Those who stand against the established system are a priori at a disadvantage, which is not removed by the toleration of their ideas, speeches, and newspapers.

Mill's passage, I drew attention to the premise hidden in this assumption: free and equal discussion can fulfill the function attributed to it only if it is *rational*—expression and development of independent thinking, free from indoctrination, manipulation, extraneous authority. The notion of pluralism and countervailing powers is no substitute for this requirement. One might in theory construct a state in which a multitude of different pressures, interests, and authorities balance each other out and result in a truly general and rational interest. However, such a construct badly fits a society in which powers are and remain unequal and even increase their unequal weight when they run their own course. It fits even worse when the variety of pressures unifies and coagulates into an overwhelming whole, integrating the particular countervailing powers by virtue of an increasing standard of living and an increasing concentration of power. Then, the laborer, whose real interest conflicts with that of management, the common consumer whose real interest conflicts with that of the producer, the intellectual whose vocation conflicts with that of his employer find themselves submitting to a system against which they are powerless and appear unreasonable. The ideas of the available alternatives evaporates into an utterly utopian dimension in which it is at home, for a free society is indeed unrealistically and undefinably different from the existing ones. Under these circumstances, whatever improvement may occur "in the normal course of events" and without subversion is likely to be improvement in the direction determined by the particular interests which control the whole.

By the same token, those minorities which strive for a change of the whole itself will, under optimal conditions which rarely prevail, be left free to deliberate and discuss, to speak and to assemble—and will be left harmless and helpless in the face of the overwhelming majority, which militates against qualitative social change. This majority is firmly grounded in the increasing satisfaction of needs, and technological and mental coordination, which testify to the general helplessness of radical groups in a well-functioning social system.

Within the affluent democracy, the affluent discussion prevails, and within the established framework, it is tolerant to a large extent. All points of view can be heard: the Communist and the Fascist, the Left and the Right, the white and the Negro, the crusaders for armament and for disarmament. Moreover, in endlessly dragging debates over the media, the stupid opinion is treated with the same respect as the intelligent one, the misinformed may talk as long as the informed, and propaganda rides along with education, truth with falsehood. This pure toleration of sense and nonsense is justified by the democratic argument that nobody, neither group nor individual, is in possession of the truth and capable of defining what is right and wrong, good and bad. Therefore, all contesting opinions must be submitted to "the people" for its deliberation and choice. But I have already suggested that the democratic argument implies a necessary condition, namely, that the people must be capable of deliberating and choosing on the basis of knowledge, that they must have access to authentic information, and that, on this basis, their evaluation must be the result of autonomous thought.

In the contemporary period, the democratic argument for abstract tolerance tends to be invalidated by the invalidation of the democratic process itself. The liberating force of democracy was the chance it gave to effective dissent, on the individual as well as social scale, its openness to qualitatively different forms of government, of culture, education, work—of the human existence in general. The toleration of free discussion and the equal right of opposites was to define and clarify the different forms of dissent: their direction, content, prospect. But with the concentration of economic and political power and the integration of opposites in a society which uses technology as an instrument of domination, effective dissent is blocked where it could freely emerge: in the formation of opinion, in information and communication, in speech and assembly. Under the rule of monopolistic media—themselves the mere instruments of economic and political power—a mentality is created for which right and wrong, true and false are predefined wherever they affect the vital interests of the society. This is, prior to all expression and communication, a matter of semantics: the blocking of effective dissent, of the recognition of that which is not of the Establishment which begins

in the language that is publicized and administered. The meaning of words is rigidly stabilized.
Rational persuasion, persuasion to the opposite is
all but precluded. The avenues of entrance are
closed to the meaning of words and ideas other
than the established one—established by the publicity of the powers that be, and verified in their
practices. Other words can be spoken and heard,
other ideas can be expressed, but, at the massive
scale of the conservative majority (outside such
enclaves as the intelligentsia), they are immediately "evaluated" (i.e. automatically understood)
in terms of the public language—a language
which determines "a priori" the direction in
which the thought process moves. Thus the
process of reflection ends where it started: in
the given conditions and relations. Self-validat-
ing, the argument of the discussion repels the
contradiction because the antithesis is redefined
in terms of the thesis. For example, thesis: we
work for peace; antithesis: we prepare for war
(or even: we wage war); unification of opposites: preparing for war *is* working for peace.
Peace is redefined as necessarily, in the prevailing situation, including preparation for war (or
even war) and in this Orwellian form, the meaning of the word "peace" is stabilized. Thus, the
basic vocabulary of the Orwellian language operates as a priori categories of understanding:
preforming all content. These conditions invali-
date the logic of tolerance which involves the
rational development of meaning and precludes
the closing of meaning. Consequently, persuasion through discussion and the equal presenta-

tion of opposites (even where it is really equal) easily lose their liberating force as factors of understanding and learning; they are far more likely to strengthen the established thesis and to repel the alternatives.

Impartiality to the utmost, equal treatment of competing and conflicting issues is indeed a basic requirement for decision-making in the democratic process—it is an equally basic requirement for defining the limits of tolerance. But in a democracy with totalitarian organization, objectivity may fulfill a very different function, namely, to foster a mental attitude which tends to obliterate the difference between true and false, information and indoctrination, right and wrong. In fact, the decision between opposed opinions has been made before the presentation and discussion get under way—made, not by a conspiracy or a sponsor or a publisher, not by any dictatorship, but rather by the "normal course of events," which is the course of administered events, and by the mentality shaped in this course. Here, too, it is the whole which determines the truth. Then the decision asserts itself, without any open violation of objectivity, in such things as the make-up of a newspaper (with the breaking up of vital information into bits interspersed between extraneous material, irrelevant items, relegating of some radically negative news to an obscure place), in the juxtaposition of gorgeous ads with unmitigated horrors, in the introduction and interruption of the broadcasting of facts by overwhelming commercials. The result is a *neutralization* of opposites, a neutralization, however, which takes place on the firm grounds of the structural limitation of tolerance and within a preformed mentality. When a magazine prints side by side a negative and a positive report on the FBI, it fulfills honestly the requirements of objectivity: however, the chances are that the positive wins because the image of the institution is deeply engraved in the mind of the people. Or, if a newscaster reports the torture and murder of civil rights workers in the same unemotional tone he uses to describe the stock-market or the weather, or with the same great emotion with which he says his commercials, then such objectivity is spurious—more, it offends against humanity and truth by being calm where one should be enraged, by refraining from accusation where accusation is in the facts themselves. The tolerance expressed in such impartiality serves to minimize or even absolve prevailing intolerance and suppression. If objectivity has anything to do with truth, and if truth is more than a matter of logic and science, then this kind of objectivity is false, and this kind of tolerance inhuman. And if it is necessary to break the established universe of meaning (and the practice enclosed in this universe) in order to enable man to find out what is true and false, this deceptive impartiality would have to be abandoned. The people exposed to this impartiality are no *tabulae rasae*, they are indoctrinated by the conditions under which they live and think and which they do not transcend. To enable them to become autonomous, to find by themselves what is true and what is false for man in the existing society, they would have to be freed from the prevailing indoctrination (which is no longer recognized as indoctrination). But this means that the trend would have to be reversed: they would have to get information slanted in the opposite direction. For the facts are never given immediately and never accessible immediately; they are established, "mediated" by those who made them; the truth, "the whole truth" surpasses these facts and requires the rupture with their appearance. This rupture—prerequisite and token of all freedom of thought and of speech—cannot be accomplished within the established framework of abstract tolerance and spurious objectivity because these are precisely the factors which precondition the mind *against* the rupture.

The factual barriers which totalitarian democracy erects against the efficacy of qualitative dissent are weak and pleasant enough compared with the practices of a dictatorship which claims to educate the people in the truth. With all its limitations and distortions, democratic tolerance is under all circumstances more humane than an institutionalized intolerance which sacrifices the rights and liberties of the living generations for the sake of future generations. The question is whether this is the only alternative. I shall presently try to suggest the direction in which an answer may be sought. In any case, the contrast is not between democracy in the abstract and dictatorship in the abstract.

Democracy is a form of government which fits very different types of society( this holds true

even for a democracy with universal suffrage
and equality before the law), and the human
costs of a democracy are always and everywhere
those exacted by the society whose government
it is. Their range extends all the way from normal exploitation, poverty, and insecurity to the
victims of wars, police actions, military aid, etc.,
in which the society is engaged—and not only to
the victims within its own frontiers. These considerations can never justify the exacting of different sacrifices and different victims on behalf
of a future better society, but they do allow
weighing the costs involved in the perpetuation
of an existing society against the risk of promot-
ing alternatives which offer a reasonable chance
of pacification and liberation. Surely, no government can be expected to foster its own subversion, but in a democracy such a right is vested
in the people (i.e. in the majority of the people).
This means that the ways should not be blocked
on which a subversive majority could develop,
and if they are blocked by organized repression
and indoctrination, their reopening may require
apparently undemocratic means. They would include the withdrawal of toleration of speech and
assembly from groups and movements which
promote aggressive policies, armament, chauvin-
ism, discrimination on the grounds of race and
religion, or which oppose the extension of public
services, social security, medical care, etc. Moreover, the restoration of freedom of thought may
necessitate new and rigid restrictions on teachings and practices in the educational institutions
which, by their very methods and concepts, serve

to enclose the mind within the established universe of discourse and behavior—thereby precluding a priori a rational evaluation of the alternatives. And to the degree to which freedom of thought involves the struggle against inhumanity, restoration of such freedom would also imply intolerance toward scientific research in the interest of deadly "deterrents," of abnormal human endurance under inhuman conditions, etc. I shall presently discuss the question as to who is to decide on the distinction between liberating and repressive, human and inhuman teachings and practices; I have already suggested that this distinction is not a matter of value-preference but of rational criteria.

While the reversal of the trend in the educational enterprise at least could conceivably be enforced by the students and teachers themselves, and thus be self-imposed, the systematic withdrawal of tolerance toward regressive and repressive opinions and movements could only be envisaged as results of large-scale pressure which would amount to an upheaval. In other words, it would presuppose that which is still to be accomplished: the reversal of the trend. However, resistance at particular occasions, boycott, non-participation at the local and small-group level may perhaps prepare the ground. The subversive character of the restoration of freedom appears most clearly in that dimension of society where false tolerance and free enterprise do perhaps the most serious and lasting damage, namely, in business and publicity. Against the emphatic insistence on the part of spokesmen for labor, I maintain that practices such as planned obsolescence, collusion between union leadership and management, slanted publicity are not simply imposed from above on a powerless rank and file, but are *tolerated* by them—and by the consumer at large. However, it would be ridiculous to speak of a possible withdrawal of tolerance with respect to these practices and to the ideologies promoted by them. For they pertain to the basis on which the repressive affluent society rests and reproduces itself and its vital defenses —their removal would be that total revolution which this society so effectively repels.

To discuss tolerance in such a society means to re-examine the issue of violence and the traditional distinction between violent and non-violent action. The discussion should not, from the beginning, be clouded by ideologies which serve the perpetuation of violence. Even in the advanced centers of civilization, violence actually prevails: it is practiced by the police, in the prisons and mental institutions, in the fight against racial minorities; it is carried, by the defenders of metropolitan freedom, into the backward countries. This violence indeed breeds violence. But to refrain from violence in the face of vastly superior violence is one thing, to renounce a priori violence against violence, on ethical or psychological grounds (because it may atagonize sympathizers) is another. Non-violence is normally not only preached to but exacted from the weak—it is a necessity rather than a virtue, and normally it does not seriously harm the case of the strong. (Is the case of India an exception?

There, passive resistance was carried through on a massive scale, which disrupted, or threatened to disrupt, the economic life of the country. Quantity turns into quality: on such a scale, passive resistance is no longer passive—it ceases to be non-violent. The same holds true for the General Strike.) Robespierre's distinction between the terror of liberty and the terror of despotism, and his moral glorification of the former belongs to the most convincingly condemned aberrations, even if the white terror was more bloody than the red terror. The comparative evaluation in terms of the number of victims is the quantifying approach which reveals the man-made horror throughout history that made violence a necessity. In terms of historical function, there is a difference between revolutionary and reactionary violence, between violence practiced by the oppressed and by the oppressors. In terms of ethics, both forms of violence are inhuman and evil—but since when is history made in accordance with ethical standards? To start applying them at the point where the oppressed rebel against the oppressors, the have-nots against the haves is serving the cause of actual violence by weakening the protest against it.

Comprenez enfin ceci: si la violence a commencé ce soir, si l'exploitation ni l'oppression n'ont jamais existé sur terre, peut-être la non-violence affichée peut apaiser la querelle. Mais si le régime tout entier et jusqu'à vos non-violentes pensées sont conditionnées par une oppression millénaire, votre passivité ne sert qu'à vous ranger du côté des oppresseurs. (Sartre, Preface to Frantz Fanon, *Les Damnés de la Terre*, Paris: Maspéro, 1961, p. 22).

The very notion of false tolerance, and the distinction between right and wrong limitations on tolerance, between progressive and regressive indoctrination, revolutionary and reactionary violence demand the statement of criteria for its validity. These standards must be prior to whatever constitutional and legal criteria are set up and applied in an existing society (such as "clear and present danger," and other established definitions of civil rights and liberties), for such definitions themselves presuppose standards of freedom and repression as applicable or not applicable in the respective society: they are specifications of more general concepts. By whom, and according to what standards, can the political distinction between true and false, progressive and regressive (for in this sphere, these pairs are equivalent) be made and its validity be justified? At the outset, I propose that the question cannot be answered in terms of the alternative between democracy and dictatorship, according to which, in the latter, one individual or group, without any effective control from below, arrogate to themselves the decision. Historically, even in the most democratic democracies, the vital and final decisions affecting the society as a whole have been made, constitutionally or in fact, by one or several groups without effective control by the people themselves. The ironical question: who educates the educators (i.e. the political leaders) also applies to democracy. The only authentic alternative and negation of dictatorship (with respect to this question) would be a society in which "the people" have become autonomous individuals, freed from the repressive requirements of a struggle for existence in the interest of domination, and as such human beings choosing their government and determining their life. Such a society does not yet exist anywhere. In the meantime, the question must be treated *in abstracto*—abstraction, not from the historical possibilities, but from the realities of the prevailing societies.

I suggested that the distinction between true and false tolerance, between progress and regression can be made rationally on empirical grounds. The real possibilities of human freedom are relative to the attained stage of civilization. They depend on the material and intellectual resources available at the respective stage, and they are quantifiable and calculable to a high degree. So are, at the stage of advanced industrial society, the most rational ways of using these resources and distributing the social product with priority on the satisfaction of vital needs and with a minimum of toil and injustice. In other words, it is possible to define the direction in which prevailing institutions, policies, opinions would have to be changed in order to improve the chance of a peace which is not identical with cold war and a little hot war, and a satisfaction of needs which does not feed on poverty, oppression, and exploitation. Consequently, it is also possible to identify policies, opinions, movements which would promote this chance, and those which would do the opposite. Suppression of the regressive ones is a prerequisite for the strengthening of the progressive ones.

The question, who is qualified to make all these distinctions, definitions, identifications for the society as a whole, has now one logical answer, namely, everyone "in the maturity of his faculties" as a human being, everyone who has learned to think rationally and autonomously. The answer to Plato's educational dictatorship is the democratic educational dictatorship of free men. John Stuart Mill's conception of the *res publica* is not the opposite of Plato's: the liberal too demands the authority of Reason not only as an intellectual but also as a political power. In Plato, rationality is confined to the small number of philosopher-kings; in Mill, every rational human being participates in the discussion and decision—but only as a rational being. Where society has entered the phase of total administration and indoctrination, this would be a small number indeed, and not necessarily that of the elected representatives of the people. The problem is not that of an educational dictatorship, but that of breaking the tyranny of public opinion and its makers in the closed society.

However, granted the empirical rationality of the distinction between progress and regression, and granted that it may be applicable to tolerance, and may justify strongly discriminatory tolerance on political grounds (cancellation of the liberal creed of free and equal discussion), another impossible consequence would follow. I said that, by virtue of its inner logic, withdrawal of tolerance from regressive movements, and discriminatory tolerance in favor of progressive tendencies would be tantamount to the "official" promotion of subversion. The historical calculus of progress (which is actually the calculus of the prospective reduction of cruelty, misery, suppression) seems to involve the calculated choice between two forms of political violence: that on the part of the legally constituted powers (by their legitimate action, or by their tacit consent, or by their inability to prevent violence), and that on the part of potentially subversive movements. Moreover, with respect to the latter, a policy of unequal treatment would protect radicalism on the Left against that on the Right. Can the historical calculus be reasonably extended to the justification of one form of violence as against another? Or better (since "justification" carries a moral connotation), is there historical evidence to the effect that the social origin and impetus of violence (from among the ruled or the ruling classes, the have or the have-nots, the Left or the Right) is in a demonstrable relation to progress (as defined above)?

With all the qualifications of a hypothesis based on an "open" historical record, it seems that the violence emanating from the rebellion of the oppressed classes broke the historical continuum of injustice, cruelty, and silence for a brief moment, brief but explosive enough to achieve an increase in the scope of freedom and justice, and a better and more equitable distribution of misery and oppression in a new social system—in one word: progress in civilization.

The English civil wars, the French Revolution, the Chinese and the Cuban Revolutions may illustrate the hypothesis. In contrast, the one historical change from one social system to another, marking the beginning of a new period in civilization, which was *not* sparked and driven by an effective movement "from below," namely, the collapse of the Roman Empire in the West, brought about a long period of regression for long centuries, until a new, higher period of civilization was painfully born in the violence of the heretic revolts of the thirteenth century and in the peasant and laborer revolts of the fourteenth century.[1]

With respect to historical violence emanating from among ruling classes, no such relation to progress seems to obtain. The long series of dynastic and imperialist wars, the liquidation of Spartacus in Germany in 1919, Fascism and Nazism did not break but rather tightened and streamlined the continuum of suppression. I said emanating "from among ruling classes": to be sure, there is hardly any organized violence from above that does not mobilize and activate mass support from below; the decisive question is, on behalf of and in the interest of which groups and institutions is such violence released? And the answer is not necessarily ex post: in the historical examples just mentioned, it could be and was anticipated whether the movement would serve

[1] In modern times, fascism has been a consequence of the transition to industrial society *without* a revolution. See Barrington Moore's *Social Origins of Dictatorship and Democracy* (Boston: Beacon Press, 1966).

the revamping of the old order or the emergence of the new.

Liberating tolerance, then, would mean intolerance against movements from the Right, and toleration of movements from the Left. As to the scope of this tolerance and intolerance: . . . it would extend to the stage of action as well as of discussion and propaganda, of deed as well as of word. The traditional criterion of clear and present danger seems no longer adequate to a stage where the whole society is in the situation of the theater audience when somebody cries: "fire." It is a situation in which the total catastrophy could be triggered off any moment, not only by a technical error, but also by a rational miscalculation of risks, or by a rash speech of one of the leaders. In past and different circumstances, the speeches of the Fascist and Nazi leaders were the immediate prologue to the massacre. The distance between the propaganda and the action, between the organization and its release on the people had become too short. But the spreading of the word could have been stopped before it was too late: if democratic tolerance had been withdrawn when the future leaders started their campaign, mankind would have had a chance of avoiding Auschwitz and a World War.

The whole post-fascist period is one of clear and present danger. Consequently, true pacification requires the withdrawal of tolerance before the deed, at the stage of communication in word, print, and picture. Such extreme suspension of the right of free speech and free assembly is in-

deed justified only if the whole of society is
in extreme danger. I maintain that our society
is in such an emergency situation, and that it has
become the normal state of affairs. Different
opinions and "philosophies" can no longer compete peacefully for adherence and persuasion on
rational grounds: the "marketplace of ideas" is
organized and delimited by those who determine
the national and the individual interest. In this
society, for which the ideologists have proclaimed the "end of ideology," the false consciousness has become the general consciousness
—from the government down to its last objects.
The small and powerless minorities which struggle against the false consciousness and its bene-
ficiaries must be helped: their continued existence is more important than the preservation of
abused rights and liberties which grant constitutional powers to those who oppress these minorities. It should be evident by now that the exercise
of civil rights by those who don't have them presupposes the withdrawal of civil rights from
those who prevent their exercise, and that liberation of the Damned of the Earth presupposes
suppression not only of their old but also of their
new masters.

Withdrawal of tolerance from regressive
movements *before* they can become active; intolerance even toward thought, opinion, and
word, and finally, intolerance in the opposite direction, that is, toward the self-styled conserva-
tives, to the political Right—these anti-democratic notions respond to the actual development of
the democratic society which has destroyed the

basis for universal tolerance. The conditions under which tolerance can again become a liberating and humanizing force have still to be created.
When tolerance mainly serves the protection
and preservation of a repressive society, when it
serves to neutralize opposition and to render
men immune against other and better forms of
life, then tolerance has been perverted. And
when this perversion starts in the mind of the
individual, in his consciousness, his needs, when
heteronomous interests occupy him before he
can experience his servitude, then the efforts to
counteract his dehumanization must begin at the
place of entrance, there where the false consciousness takes form (or rather: is systematically
formed)—it must begin with stopping the words
and images which feed this consciousness. To
be sure, this is censorship, even precensorship,
but openly directed against the more or less hidden censorship that permeates the free media.
Where the false consciousness has become prevalent in national and popular behavior, it trans-
lates itself almost immediately into practice:
the safe distance between ideology and reality,
repressive thought and repressive action, between the word of destruction and the deed of
destruction is dangerously shortened. Thus, the
break through the false consciousness may provide the Archimedean point for a larger emancipation—at an infinitesimally small spot, to be
sure, but it is on the enlargement of such small
spots that the chance of change depends.

The forces of emancipation cannot be identified with any social class which, by virtue of its

material condition, is free from false consciousness. Today, they are hopelessly dispersed throughout the society, and the fighting minorities and isolated groups are often in opposition to their own leadership. In the society at large, the mental space for denial and reflection must first be recreated. Repulsed by the concreteness of the administered society, the effort of emancipation becomes "abstract"; it is reduced to facilitating the recognition of what is going on, to freeing language from the tyranny of the Orwellian syntax and logic, to developing the concepts that comprehend reality. More than ever, the proposition holds true that progress in freedom demands progress in the *consciousness* of freedom. Where the mind has been made into a subject-object of politics and policies, intellectual autonomy, the realm of "pure" thought has become a matter of *political education* (or rather: counter-education).

This means that previously neutral, value-free, formal aspects of learning and teaching now become, on their own grounds and in their own right, political: learning to know the facts, the whole truth, and to comprehend it is radical criticism throughout, intellectual subversion. In a world in which the human faculties and needs are arrested or perverted, autonomous thinking leads into a "perverted world": contradiction and counter-image of the established world of repression. And this contradiction is not simply stipulated, is not simply the product of confused thinking or phantasy, but is the logical development of the given, the existing world. To the degree to which this development is actually impeded by the sheer weight of a repressive society and the necessity of making a living in it, repression invades the academic enterprise itself, even prior to all restrictions on academic freedom. The pre-empting of the mind vitiates impartiality and objectivity: unless the student learns to think in the opposite direction, he will be inclined to place the facts into the predominant framework of values. Scholarship, i.e. the acquisition and communication of knowledge, prohibits the purification and isolation of facts from the context of the whole truth. An essential part of the latter is recognition of the frightening extent to which history was made and recorded by and for the victors, that is, the extent to which history was the development of oppression. And this oppression is in the facts themselves which it establishes; thus they themselves carry a negative value as part and aspect of their facticity. To treat the great crusades *against* humanity (like that against the Albigensians) with the same impartiality as the desperate struggles *for* humanity means neutralizing their opposite historical function, reconciling the executioners with their victims, distorting the record. Such spurious neutrality serves to reproduce acceptance of the dominion of the victors in the consciousness of man. Here, too, in the education of those who are not yet maturely integrated, in the mind of the young, the ground for liberating tolerance is still to be created.

Education offers still another example of spurious, abstract tolerance in the guise of con-

creteness and truth: it is epitomized in the concept of self-actualization. From the permissiveness of all sorts of license to the child, to the constant psychological concern with the personal
problems of the student, a large-scale movement
is under way against the evils of repression and
the need for being oneself. Frequently brushed
aside is the question as to what has to be re-
pressed before one can be a self, oneself. The individual potential is first a negative one, a portion
of the potential of his society: of aggression,
guilt feeling, ignorance, resentment, cruelty
which vitiate his life instincts. If the identity of
the self is to be more than the immediate realization of this potential (undesirable for the individual as human being), then it requires repression and sublimation, conscious transformation.
This process involves at each stage (to use the
ridiculed terms which here reveal their succinct
concreteness) the negation of the negation,
mediation of the immediate, and identity is no
more and no less than this process. "Alienation"
is the constant and essential element of identity,
the objective side of the subject—and not, as it
is made to appear today, a disease, a psychological condition. Freud well knew the difference
between progressive and regressive, liberating
and destructive repression. The publicity of self-
actualization promotes the removal of the one
and the other, it promotes existence in that immediacy which, in a repressive society, is (to use
another Hegelian term) bad immediacy
(*schlechte Unmittelbarkeit*). It isolates the individual from the one dimension where he could

"find himself": from his political existence, which is at the core of his entire existence. Instead, it encourages non-conformity and letting-go in ways which leave the real engines of repression in the society entirely intact, which even strengthen these engines by substituting the satisfactions of private and personal rebellion for a more than private and personal, and therefore more authentic, opposition. The desublimation involved in this sort of self-actualization is itself repressive inasmuch as it weakens the necessity and the power of the intellect, the catalytic force of that unhappy consciousness which does not revel in the archetypal personal release of frustration—hopeless resurgence of the Id which will sooner or later succumb to the omnipresent rationality of the administered world—but which recognizes the horror of the whole in the most private frustration and actualizes itself in this recognition.

I have tried to show how the changes in advanced democratic societies, which have undermined the basis of economic and political liberalism, have also altered the liberal function of tolerance. The tolerance which was the great achievement of the liberal era is still professed and (with strong qualifications) practiced, while the economic and political process is subjected to an ubiquitous and effective administration in accordance with the predominant interests. The result is an objective contradiction between the economic and political structure on the one side, and the theory and practice of toleration on the other. The altered social structure tends to weaken the effectiveness of tolerance toward dissenting and oppositional movements and to strengthen conservative and reactionary forces. Equality of tolerance becomes abstract, spurious. With the actual decline of dissenting forces in the society, the opposition is insulated in small and frequently antagonistic groups who, even where tolerated within the narrow limits set by the hierarchical structure of society, are powerless while they keep within these limits. But the tolerance shown to them is deceptive and promotes coordination. And on the firm foundations of a coordinated society all but closed against qualitative change, tolerance itself serves to contain such change rather than to promote it.

These same conditions render the critique of such tolerance abstract and academic, and the proposition that the balance between tolerance toward the Right and toward the Left would have to be radically redressed in order to restore the liberating function of tolerance becomes only an unrealistic speculation. Indeed, such a redressing seems to be tantamount to the establishment of a "right of resistance" to the point of subversion. There is not, there cannot be any such right for any group or individual against a constitutional government sustained by a majority of the population. But I believe that there is a "natural right" of resistance for oppressed and overpowered minorities to use extralegal means if the legal ones have proved to be inadequate. Law and order are always and everywhere the law and order which protect the established hierarchy; it is nonsensical to invoke the absolute authority of this law and this order against those who suffer from it and struggle against it —not for personal advantages and revenge, but for their share of humanity. There is no other judge over them than the constituted authorities, the police, and their own conscience. If they use violence, they do not start a new chain of violence but try to break an established one. Since they will be punished, they know the risk, and when they are willing to take it, no third person, and least of all the educator and intellectual, has the right to preach them abstention.

## POSTSCRIPT 1968

UNDER the conditions prevailing in this country, tolerance does not, and cannot, fulfill the civilizing function attributed to it by the liberal protagonists of democracy, namely, protection of dissent. The progressive historical force of tolerance lies in its extension to those modes and forms of dissent which are not committed to the status quo of society, and not confined to the institutional framework of the established society. Consequently, the idea of tolerance implies the necessity, for the dissenting group or individuals, to become illegitimate if and when the established legitimacy prevents and counteracts the development of dissent. This

would be the case not only in a totalitarian society, under a dictatorship, in one-party states, but
also in a democracy (representative, parliament-
ary, or "direct") where the majority does not
result from the development of independent
thought and opinion but rather from the monopolistic or oligopolistic administration of public
opinion, without terror and (normally) without
censorship. In such cases, the majority is self-
perpetuating while perpetuating the vested interests which *made* it a majority. In its very
structure this majority is "closed," petrified; it
repels "a priori" any change other than changes
within the system. But this means that the majority is no longer justified in claiming the democratic title of the best guardian of the common
interest. And such a majority is all but the opposite of Rousseau's "general will": it is composed, not of individuals who, in their political
functions, have made effective "abstraction"
from their private interests, but, on the contrary,
of individuals who have effectively identified
their private interests with their political functions. And the representatives of this majority, in
ascertaining and executing its will, ascertain and
execute the will of the vested interests which
have formed the majority. The ideology of
democracy hides its lack of substance.

In the United States, this tendency goes hand
in hand with the monopolistic or oligopolistic
concentration of capital in the formation of public opinion, i.e., of the majority. The chance of
influencing, in any effective way, this majority
is at a price, in dollars, totally out of reach of the

radical opposition. Here too, free competition and exchange of ideas have become a farce. The Left has no equal voice, no equal access to the mass media and their public facilities—not because a conspiracy excludes it, but because, in good old capitalist fashion, it does not have the required purchasing power. And the Left does not have the purchasing power because it is the Left. These conditions impose upon the radical minorities a strategy which is in essence a refusal to allow the continuous functioning of allegedly indiscriminate but in fact discriminate tolerance, for example, a strategy of protesting against the alternate matching of a spokesman for the Right (or Center) with one for the Left. Not "equal" but *more* representation of the Left would be equalization of the prevailing inequality.

Within the solid framework of preestablished inequality and power, tolerance is practiced indeed. Even outrageous opinions are expressed, outrageous incidents are televised; and the critics of established policies are interrupted by the same number of commercials as the conservative advocates. Are these interludes supposed to counteract the sheer weight, magnitude, and continuity of system-publicity, indoctrination which operates playfully through the endless commercials as well as through the entertainment?

Given this situation, I suggested in "Repressive Tolerance" the practice of discriminating tolerance in an inverse direction, as a means of shifting the balance between Right and Left by restraining the liberty of the Right, thus counteracting the pervasive inequality of freedom (unequal opportunity of access to the means of democratic persuasion) and strengthening the oppressed against the oppressors. Tolerance would be restricted with respect to movements of a demonstrably aggressive or destructive character (destructive of the prospects for peace, justice, and freedom for all). Such discrimination would also be applied to movements opposing the extension of social legislation to the poor, weak, disabled. As against the virulent denunciations that such a policy would do away with the sacred liberalistic principle of equality for "the other side," I maintain that there are issues where either there is no "other side" in any more than a formalistic sense, or where "the other side" is demonstrably "regressive" and impedes possible improvement of the human condition. To tolerate propaganda for inhumanity vitiates the goals not only of liberalism but of every progressive political philosophy.

I presupposed the existence of demonstrable criteria for aggressive, regressive, destructive forces. If the final democratic criterion of the declared opinion of the majority no longer (or rather not yet) prevails, if vital ideas, values, and ends of human progress no longer (or rather not yet) enter, as competing equals, the formation of public opinion, if the people are no longer (or rather not yet) sovereign but "made" by the real sovereign powers—is there any alternative other than the dictatorship of an "elite" over the people? For the opinion of people (usually designated as The People) who are unfree in the

very faculties in which liberalism saw the roots
of freedom: independent thought and independent speech, can carry no overriding validity and
authority—even if The People constitute the
overwhelming majority.

If the choice were between genuine democracy and dictatorship, democracy would certainly be preferable. But democracy does not
prevail. The radical critics of the existing political process are thus readily denounced as advo-
cating an "elitism," a dictatorship of intellectuals
as an alternative. What we have in fact is government, representative government by a non-intel-
lectual minority of politicians, generals, and
businessmen. The record of this "elite" is not
very promising, and political prerogatives for
the intelligentsia may not necessarily be worse
for the society as a whole.

In any case, John Stuart Mill, not exactly an
enemy of liberal and representative government,
was not so allergic to the political leadership of
the intelligentsia as the contemporary guardians
of semi-democracy are. Mill believed that "individual mental superiority" justifies "reckoning
one person's opinion as equivalent to more than
one":

> Until there shall have been devised, and until
> opinion is willing to accept, some mode of
> plural voting which may assign to education
> as such the degree of superior influence due to
> it, and sufficient as a counterpoise to the
> numerical weight of the least educated class,
> for so long the benefits of completely univer-
> sal suffrage cannot be obtained without bring-

ing with them, as it appears to me, more than equivalent evils.[1]

"Distinction in favor of education, right in itself," was also supposed to preserve "the educated from the class legislation of the uneducated," without enabling the former to practice a class legislation of their own.[2]

Today, these words have understandably an antidemocratic, "elitist" sound—understandably because of their dangerously radical implications. For if "education" is more and other than training, learning, preparing for the existing society, it means not only enabling man to know and understand the facts which make up reality but also to know and understand the factors that establish the facts so that he can change their inhuman reality. And such humanistic education would involve the "hard" sciences ("hard" as in the "hardware" bought by the Pentagon?), would free them from their destructive direction. In other words, such education would indeed badly serve the Establishment, and to give political prerogatives to the men and women thus educated would indeed be anti-democratic in the terms of the Establishment. But these are not the only terms.

However, the alternative to the established semi-democratic process is *not* a dictatorship or elite, no matter how intellectual and intelligent, but the struggle for a real democracy. Part of

[1]*Considerations on Representative Government* (Chicago: Gateway Edition, 1962), p. 183.

[2]*Ibid.*, p. 181.

this struggle is the fight against an ideology of tolerance which, in reality, favors and fortifies the conservation of the status quo of inequality and discrimination. For this struggle, I proposed the practice of discriminating tolerance. To be sure, this practice already presupposes the radical goal which it seeks to achieve. I committed this *petitio principii* in order to combat the pernicious ideology that tolerance is already institutionalized in this society. The tolerance which is the life element, the token of a free society, will never be the gift of the powers that be; it can, under the prevailing conditions of tyranny by the majority, only be won in the sustained effort of radical minorities, willing to break this tyranny and to work for the emergence of a free and sovereign majority—minorities intolerant, militantly intolerant and disobedient to the rules of behavior which tolerate destruction and suppression.

19/12/79